Shinto

A Celebration of Life

First published by O-Books, 2010
O Books is an imprint of John Hunt Publishing Ltd., The Bothy, Deershot Lodge, Park Lane, Ropley,
Hants, SO24 0BE, UK
office1@o-books.net
www.o-books.com

Distribution in:	South Africa
UK and Europe	Stephan Phillips (pty) Ltd
Orca Book Services Ltd	Email: orders@stephanphillips.com
	Tel: 27 21 4489839 Telefax: 27 21 4479879

Home trade orders
tradeorders@orcabookservices.co.uk
Tel: 01235 465521 Fax: 01235 465555

Text copyright Aidan Rankin 2010

ISBN: 978 1 84694 438 3

Export orders
exportorders@orcabookservices.co.uk
Tel: 01235 465516 or 01235 465517
Fax: 01235 465555

USA and Canada
NBN
custserv@nbnbooks.com
Tel: 1 800 462 6420 Fax: 1 800 338 4550

Australia and New Zealand
Brumby Books
sales@brumbybooks.com.au
Tel: 61 3 9761 5535 Fax: 61 3 9761 7095

Far East (offices in Singapore, Thailand,
Hong Kong, Taiwan)
Pansing Distribution Pte Ltd
kemal@pansing.com
Tel: 65 6319 9939 Fax: 65 6462 5761

A CIP catalogue record for this book is
available from the British Library.

Printed in the UK by CPI Antony Rowe
Printed in the USA by Offset Paperback Mfrs,
Inc

We operate a distinctive and ethical publishing philosophy in all
areas of its business, from its global network of authors to
production and worldwide distribution.

Shinto

A Celebration of Life

Aidan Rankin

BOOKS

Winchester, UK
Washington, USA

Contents

For BGS

'Nature is not a place to visit. It is home.'

Gary Snyder, The Practice of the Wild (2004).

Tomoe: The Sacred Swirl

The *Tomoe*, often referred to as *Mistu-Tomoe*, is one of the most visible symbols of Shinto today. Tomoe (pronounced 'Toh-mo-ay') can be translated as 'comma', with Mitsu-Tomoe as 'three commas' or 'triple comma'. The word also has the connotation of 'swirl' or circular motion, sometimes rendered as eddy or whirlpool.

Each comma shape represents an aspect of the cosmic life force and the circle uniting them represents the interaction and interdependence of the processes that give rise to life. In Shinto, the concept of life includes both the material and spiritual dimensions, between which there are no fixed boundaries.

The three commas depict the 'visible' manifestations of the soul: its creative, calm and turbulent aspects. The spaces between the commas signify that which is hidden, mysterious and abstract in the universe. They mark the meeting point: the place where the different aspects of the soul (or the universe) interact and overlap. The circle represents perpetual motion, the constant cycles of life, death and renewal that govern all aspects of the universe, including divine forces.

Therefore it follows that the Mitsu-Tomoe also represents the High Plain of Heaven, the Earth and the Underworld. The spaces between them denote contact and overlap between these three levels of existence. The circle the process of interaction, and the center is the eternal source of creativity and wisdom, the point of origin for all life. In Shinto, the heavenly plain and the shadow-world, or Underworld, can be interpreted as aspects of consciousness, or as parallel universes.

The Tomoe has profound roots in Japanese culture. It is a development of the *Magatama* ('curved ball' or benevolent force, soul or spirit), a comma-shaped ornament found in burial mounds as early as 13000 BCE. The Magatama was a talisman of good fortune and the banishment of evil, possibly connected to similar Korean symbols for the embryo in the mother's womb, thus representing blessings and life. The Magatama became associated with Amaterasu, the Shinto sun goddess, who is the ancestor of humanity and the source of life on Earth.

The Tomoe can itself be seen as a solar symbol, related to the *svastika* of the Hindus and Jains, with its many European and Native American counterparts. The Mitsu-Tomoe closely resembles three-headed Celtic variants of the svastika. Tomoe images also exist in four-headed form, very similar to the Basque *Lauburu*, which signifies prosperity and health. Two-headed versions also call to mind the Yin-Yang symbol of Daoism. The Tomoe can be seen as the Shinto version of a universal life symbol. Ultimately, it represents *Musubi*, the cyclical process of organic growth, contraction and regeneration that governs everything in the cosmos.

Tomoe image courtesy of the Japanese Dutch Shinzen Foundation.

Acknowledgements

The writing of this book would not even have been contemplated without the help and support of the Japanese Dutch Shinzen Foundation. I am especially indebted to its Chairman and Vice Chair, respectively Professor Fons Elders and Madeleine Wardenaar, MA, and its Director, Paul de Leeuw, MA. Their insights, practical support and generous hospitality have inspired me to explore the Shinto tradition and helped me understand its relevance to the whole of humanity.

Paul is a *Kannushi*, a role that has traditionally been translated as 'Shinto priest'. However the word 'priest' does not convey the true character of his role. In one sense, it is too much: Paul does not claim that his knowledge gives him divine authority over others or the right to impose his own doctrinal version of Shinto. On the contrary, his own experiential training enables him to act as a conduit for the power of *Kami*. In Shinto, Kami is at once the divine presence and the life force pervading and connecting together everything in the universe.

Shinto's aim is to awaken us to something larger than our immediate selves, so that we become aware of our connections – social and ecological – with the rest of humanity and the natural world. Through this awareness, we encounter our true selves. Yet another, equally important, purpose is to alert us to the myriad possibilities contained in the universe, so that we learn to think, reason and feel for ourselves, have confidence in our thoughts and feelings and seek to realize our full potential as human beings. Thus in Shinto there is no division between the individual and social realms, between our personal responsibilities and our social obligations, which include obligations to nature, as the creative expression of Kami.

In this sense, the Kannushi has a wider – or at least a very different – role from that which we have come to ascribe to a priest.

He or she enables us to reach into the unconscious, to integrate the world of dreams with our waking lives so that we recognize both as aspects or levels of 'reality'. The Kannushi helps us to access our social conscience as well, so that we connect spiritual development with working towards a more just society and co-operating with the Earth rather than trying to 'conquer' it for ourselves. The integration of our rational and intuitive powers, which is the Kannushi's true role, has implications for every aspect of our lives and for the way we organize our human community. The Kannushi could be said to be a modern Shaman. Or, to express it less baldly but more accurately, his role is that of the shaman evolved over the centuries to meet the needs of an urban and increasingly techno-logical society. Rather than priest (or shaman), Paul prefers the designation Shinto Master (*Shintomeester* in Dutch) as this conveys better to westerners the experience of being a Kannushi.

Paul de Leeuw has studied extensively in Japan and introduced Shinto to the spiritually hungry soil of Europe. I have had the pleasurable and, in the true sense of the word, educational experience of working with him on the English version of *The Essence of Shinto* by Grand Master (*Kanchou*) Yamakage Motohisa, who presides over one of the oldest schools of Shinto in Japan and is Paul's initiator. I therefore offer my thanks to Grand Master Yamakage as the intellectual and spiritual ancestor of this project. And in the true spirit of Shinto, I would also like to thank my mother and father, Anne and David Rankin, for their love and encouragement.

John Hunt, my publisher, was as always positive and gently encouraging throughout as were his colleagues at O Books. I thank all of them for making this book possible.

Last, but by no means least, I would like to thank Brian Scoltock for all his practical help and moral support, and for putting up with me in both London and Yorkshire while I was hard at work on this book and probably talking about it far too much.

I hope that this book will be a worthy reflection of the creative spirit of Kami, which exists within us all.

Introduction

It is often said of Chinese and Japanese painting that what is not there is at least as important as what is. The broad brushstrokes convey with great sensitivity the *idea* of the snow-capped mountain, or the mist-shrouded valley, or the fields, streams and trees below. They give the viewer the essence of the scene, but the imagination is left to supply much of the detail. And yet the painting is far more than an outline. It explores the inner reality.

This book attempts to do the same with Shinto, the native faith of the Japanese. For in Shinto, as in its better known Chinese counterpart, Taoism (or Daoism), what is omitted is also as important as what is specifically included. Shinto is a sensibility before it is a philosophy. It is a way of looking at the world that allies ethics with aesthetics. The way of nature is inherently benign and works for our benefit when we understand and accommodate ourselves to it. Therefore the purpose of all ethics, all spiritual practice, is to understand the way of nature and work with it.

That philosophy of life is very different from the mainstream western approach. Over the last five hundred years especially, the west has has viewed nature as something external and threatening, something 'other' that human beings must confront, suppress or shield themselves from. 'Conquering' nature has been seen as an indication of human strength. However this view is increasingly challenged by the physical and psychological effects of environmental pollution, evidence of growing and dangerous climatic instability and a diminution in the quality of life, despite rising living standards for some. It is realized increasingly that Great Nature (as Shinto calls it) is stronger and wiser than humanity on its own and that our 'conquest' or mastery of the natural world is a dangerous illusion.

More than that, it is sensed that humanity's attempt to

1

separate itself from nature is the result of misguided political and religious dogmas. Far from being set apart from nature, we are a part of it. When we attempt to separate ourselves, we make ourselves more vulnerable rather than gaining in strength. True development or progress, we now know, means finding a new accommodation with the rest of nature and being aware of our limits as well as our potential. Within this framework, we have the possibility of living more creative and satisfying – and more ecologically sensitive – lives than in a society where economic growth and competition (with each other and with nature) have become ends in themselves. And, ironically, the science that has been used for so long as evidence for humanity's special status and right to dominate nature is showing us the extent to which all life is interlinked. The destinies of all life forms (including micro-organisms which have previously been dismissed as primitive and inconsequential) are bound up with our own fate as a species.

These insights are merely a beginning. They require a change in philosophy and a change in the way we organize our lives. That includes a questioning of some of the most basic assumptions we have made about society, politics, economics and faith. Our civilization has turned full circle as reasoned science confirms our spiritual intuitions. At the same time, the obsession with consumption and material possessions, fuelled by growth-based economics, is proving increasingly to be a dead end. Dissatisfaction with the over-emphasis on material aspects of life has induced an increasing hunger for the spiritual dimension. These intuitions, ecological and spiritual, have not yet been translated into significant action. We know, or rather *feel*, that we must change direction, but we are far less clear about *how* to do so. Shinto does not provide a blueprint for action or tell us what to do. But where it can help us, in the west, is in providing a structure or loose framework that enables us to approach human problems in a different way. This is so whether the problems are social, spiritual or environmental. From the perspective of Shinto, these categories have the same origin. They are not distinct but overlap and shade into each other.

Increasing anxiety about where we are going as a civilization has prompted a resurgence of interest in the indigenous faith traditions and spiritual pathways. Throughout the industrialized world, there is widespread interest in the traditions of Native Americans and Australian Aborigines, in African traditional traditions and the nature-centered, polytheistic faiths of ancient Europe. All these hold up a critical mirror to our civilization as well as profound ecological and social insights. They can teach us much about where we have gone wrong and what we have lost in our rush towards technological development and material gain. Yet Shinto has, perhaps, one advantage over them. The advantage is that it is a living tradition, which has evolved without interruption over millennia of human existence. Unlike other indigenous traditions, it has not been destroyed or interrupted. It was never frozen in time but has become an integral part of one of the most technologically advanced societies on Earth. Shinto reminds us that society of its ancient roots and the continuities between urban men and women and the world of Great Nature. In that sense, it is like the blades of grass that arise between the cracks in city paving stones, a reminder that everything made by humans is transient but that the principle of life is constant and continuous.

Shinto is, in a literal sense, a celebration of life. It has little to say about death and the afterlife, far less than Buddhism or Christianity, for example. It is concerned with the processes of life, from the life cycle of each individual being to the evolutionary cycle itself. If there can be said to be a founding principle of Shinto, it is the relationship between the two. That is to say, the individual life form is unique and worthy of respect in its own right, but it is also a part of the collective life of Great Nature. The same is true of the relationship between the individual and the rest of human society. Each human life is sacred, but cannot exist or fulfill itself without the rest of humanity. There is no distinction or 'choice' between individual freedom and social responsibility, individual fulfillment and the welfare of the whole. All human beings, like all other living systems, are interconnected. Human society is itself an ecosystem, which remains viable only when it is in tune with natural principles.

In the west, we are beginning to grasp more clearly that the workings of the natural world, including evolution, involve cooperation and connectedness at least as much as competition or dog-eat-dog struggle. It is the former that ensures the continuity of the life process, whereas the latter is usually detrimental. Our present ecological problems are triggered largely by human beings behaving as if they were in competition with the rest of nature, and each other. Shinto has always understood this, which is why its spiritual practice is primarily about aligning humanity with nature. Rather than preach original sin or induce guilt, it aims to induce a sense of wonder, humility and openness.

This book is not a history of Shinto. Instead, it seeks to introduce the reader to three of the most important ideas associated with the Way of Kami, as Japan's native faith is more often known. The aim is to present an alternative way of thinking, from which we can draw inspiration as we change our social and environmental priorities. It presents a holistic vision of spirituality in which the sacred is found within and around us, rather than only in other dimensions. There is, doubtless, much that is left out which further reading – and intuitive power – can fill in.

The first of the three Shinto concepts explored in this volume is Kami. This is a more subtle and complex, and yet in other ways far easier idea than gods or God. Shinto is the Way of Kami, because Kami power is found in Great Nature and within each one of us, if we allow ourselves access to it. Kannagara, the second concept, is the process of tuning in to that Kami power and learning to live with the principle of nature. The third concept, Musubi, is the most important because it encompasses both the others and gives them life. Musubi is the principle of organic growth, according to which everything in the universe behaves, including Kami. It is the cycles of life themselves and the principles that animate them. Musubi represents continuity, from epoch to epoch, generation to generation, and at the same time the continuous processes of adaptation and improvement, dying off and rebirth in new forms. Musubi is the threads that connect everything in the web of life and the principle of co-operation that binds human beings together. Musubi is integral to Shinto and yet exists independently of it and is accessible to people of all cultures and faith. It is a survival of the earliest human insights, but is also an effective spiritual counterpart to modern science.

Today's 'green' awakening is really an awareness of Musubi and an understanding of this ancient idea would give greater strength and substance to ecological consciousness. Finally, Musubi is the spiritual union of humanity and Kami. This is not an abstract or other-worldly idea, as it might initially sound. For this union takes place through all forms of human creativity, whether they are artistic or musical, philosophical or literary. Musubi is expressed equally through friendship, fellowship and love, in other words all that makes human existence truly worthwhile.

Shinto is a life-affirming faith that embraces tradition and innovation equally and helps us to reconnect with nature. It is a spiritual pathway for our time.

Chapter One: The Unbroken Thread

Shinto offers a path to Kami to men and women of all traditions and backgrounds.
Yamakage Motohisa, 79th Grand Master of Yamakage Shinto

An Indigenous Faith, A Universal Pathway

Shinto is the native faith of the Japanese people. It has ancient roots, being descended directly from spiritual practices dating back to at least 14,000 BCE. Therefore as long as there has been human habitation of the Japanese islands, there has been 'Shinto'. But it was not always called 'Shinto' and even today the term is more often used in the west than in Japan. The original Shinto was a wide variety of folk practices associated with region, tribe, extended family and community. These remain the most authentic expressions of Shinto practice. This is because in Shinto a rock formation, a freezing waterfall, a snow-capped mountain, a forest or even an ordinary-looking tree can be points of connection with divine power or the spirit world. The original Shinto was highly local, but it was also universal – an aspect of primal spirituality that saw nature as the gateway to something higher than oneself and reminded humanity to live as if nature mattered.

Shinto became a more unified system as Japan itself became a more centralized power. The earliest Chinese historical accounts of Japan, from 57 CE, refer to it as the land of Wa, a loose federation of more than a hundred tribal communities without a written script or a central government. This situation changed quite dramatically over the next five centuries, much of that change arising through Chinese and Korean influence in cultural and religious as well as political and economic spheres. The foundations for the imperial state were laid in those centuries and this process is reflected in the two publications of greatest importance to Shinto: the *Kojiki* (Record of Ancient Matters) in 712 and the *Nihongi* (Chronicles of Japan) of 720.

These two volumes are not equivalents of the Bible, Torah or Koran, or even the Bhagavad Gita. They are more like the Norse *Eddas*, in that they are compilations of myths, tales and descriptions to act as points of cultural reference rather than as articles of faith. In the Nihongi especially, these are linked to the history of Japan and its emergence as an empire. Shinto is established as a cultural background as much as a spiritual tradition.

This version of Shinto is thereby very different, at one level, from the tribal forms of spirituality from which it emerged. It is hierarchical, centered on the Emperor as a spiritual unifier as well as Head of State – the Emperor has, famously (or infamously) at times been regarded as deity in his own right, descended from the Sun Goddess Amaterasu. 'State Shinto' has been associated with national identity, as opposed to 'Folk Shinto' which is associated with local cultures and identities – and beyond that universal human spirituality.

But at another level, Shinto has remained the same. For example the Sun Goddess, who has for many centuries been seen as the center of the Shinto pantheon, is the personification of solar power, which gives life to the Earth. Her worship is the continuation of an ancient solar cult, and it also marks the deep affinity with the natural world that has persisted through the development of a literate culture and urban economy. Also, she represents the continued centrality of the feminine principle in spiritual practice, and the association of that principle with nature and life. The ancient converges with the modern in a way that is now highly relevant to us, from a western standpoint. Scientific evidence, along with the problems caused by pollution and over-consumption which we all feel in our daily lives, has made us realize that we must re-evaluate our relationship with the environment. A parallel imbalance in human relationships is making us see the need to move towards a post-patriarchal society. Shinto shows that both male and female principles can be honored and valued, and that the most ancient forms of religious worship are compatible with a modern, technologically advanced civilization – indeed more relevant than ever.

There is a pattern within Shinto of continuous adaptation while maintaining its essential characteristics. Through the centuries, it has absorbed many ideas from Buddhism, Daoism and Confucianism, imported from China and Korea, as well as from secular science and art. These influences are seen as enriching and part of spiritual evolution, rather than a challenge or a threat. Since the introduction of Buddhism to Japan in the 6th century CE, the relationship between these two faiths, in particular, has been one of creative tension and interaction. Down the centuries there have inevitably been instances of conflict and rivalry, but the overall history has been one of co-operation and cross-fertilization. The persistence and durability of the relationship offers us a model for religious diversity and mutual acceptance between faiths. The whole Shinto world-view is about adaptation, tolerance and pluralism: circularity, rather than polarity, both/and in place of either/or.

Like almost all spiritual paths, Shinto has on occasion been abused or manipulated for sinister ends. During World War II, especially, Shinto imagery was used by an oppressive and expansionist regime, much as images from ancient Germanic religion were expropriated by the Nazis. In Europe and North America today, both Christian and pagan imagery are routinely manipulated by the political right to justify racial and other prejudices. This process of defiling does not in itself invalidate those traditions. The propaganda produced by the right has nothing really to do with Christianity or paganism, except for a superficial resemblance created by stolen images. In the same way, there was nothing 'Shinto' about Japanese militarism, just as there is nothing 'Buddhist' about the military dictatorship in power in Burma at this time of writing. The Japanese martial tradition has, if anything, a closer relationship to Buddhist practice, as a development of the ascetic ideal, the cultivation of inner discipline and the tradition of the spiritual warrior. Shinto is associated with an aesthetic rejection of these values in favor of 'softer' virtues, such as appreciation of natural beauty as a value in itself.

One of the practices of greatest importance to Shinto practitioners is known as *Misogi* or purification. This involves the purifying of the body: many Shinto rituals revolve around bathing and the Shinto ethos has made strict cleanliness very much a part of Japanese popular culture. Yet these purification rituals are symbolic of the purification of the mind and heart, a process of washing away spiritual pollution and through that reinventing oneself, which means surrendering to the true self. There is perhaps a parallel with Christian baptism, especially the baptism of mature adults by some Protestant denominations. The crucial difference is that in Shinto there is no concept of 'sin'. Pollution, both physical and ethical, is merely an error to be put right through purifying the body. Nobody and nothing is 'damned'.

Another way of looking at purification within Shinto is that it recognizes and accepts the imperfections of life as much as its goodness, and our weakness and fragility as much as our creativity and strength. Nature might be great, but greatness is not the same as perfection, and one of our main errors as humans is to try to perfect everything, including ourselves, according to whatever transient and flawed vision of perfection is fashionable at the time. Misogi is a recognition at one level that 'to err is human' – we have mistaken ideas and make wrong decisions and choices at various stages of our lives, and this is just as much part of the process as spiritual growth as our positive choices. False values often coexist with life-affirming values, our motives are often mixed, and our compassionate feelings give way to anger and frustration. Misogi acknowledges the complexity of human nature, its great qualities and also its vulnerability. It allows us gracefully to accept the 'impurities' of accumulated error so that we can also appreciate our good qualities and bring them to the fore. By –literally – washing away our impurity (the physical process symbolizing the parallel spiritual process), we are able to clear our minds of destructive thoughts, regrets and, above all, a sense of guilt that is pointless and counter-productive. As the source of life, Kami contains all the positive and negative qualities associated with life, and Kami deities perform purification rites as much as the earthly beings who invoke them.

At a second level, Misogi recognizes that the process of life can make us physically and mentally exhausted, just as much as it can uplift and inspire us. Shinto is eternally conscious of the continuous cycles within nature, and cycles are characterized by downward and upward movements. Without the latter, the former become impossible. Purification is a means by which, as living systems, we renew or refresh ourselves. It is a means by which we 'recharge our batteries' at the spiritual plane, as well as mentally and physically. Misogi can be seen as a form of holiday for the spirit, which in Shinto is our life-force, our animating principle or Kami within. The spirit is purified through the cleansing of the body and the purging from the mind of toxins such as anger, resentment and delusions of grandeur. Shinto is free of neurotic sexual puritanism or the view of the body as a vehicle for 'sin': the body and sexuality are both held to be valuable, life-affirming and so inherently good. Equally, Shinto is free of neurotic fears about death, which see the body as a source of 'decay'. The death of the body is part of the overall process of life which continues in manifold forms. A dead body sinks into the earth, from which new life will spring. Misogi teaches us, as conscious, reasoning human beings, to 'accept the rough with the smooth', be aware of the negative aspects of being human (such as exhaustion, illness and death) and integrate them in our experience. At the same time, it allows us to renew and work with our most creative powers and above all to live more lightly, with fewer fears and unrealistic expectations, greater acceptance and equanimity.

In Japan, organized Shinto has reinvigorated itself over the past half century by returning to its roots - decentralized and based around self-governing shrines loosely linked by the *Jinja Honcho* or Shrine Association. However a *Jinja* that is not part of the shrine association is no less 'Shinto' than one that is. Shinto allows for copious amounts of experimentation and borrowing. Being more a sensibility than an ideology, it has no centralized list of beliefs that have to be accepted or rejected. For example, many Shinto practitioners use Yin-Yang imagery, based on the Daoist concept of two polarities or complementary principles, such as hot and cold, hard and soft, masculine and feminine, light and dark, positive and negative, mountain and valley, Heaven and Earth. Yang represents the harder, and at the same time more abstract energy, associated with mountains, heavenly power and pure intellect. Yin represents the softer, more earth-centered energy, associated with valleys, subtle powers and intuition. Each of these principles, crucially, contains an element of the other and together they make up the whole. Neither polarity makes sense or is complete on its own. An over-emphasis on one (at the expense of the other) produces imbalances, whether physical and psychological within individuals, or social and political within the larger human community.

Yin and Yang are not hostile poles, but complements that continuously and creatively interact. This is why they are represented in a circular symbol that has become increasingly popular in the west, as it is understood increasingly that we have emphasized the Yang to the detriment of the Yin, and that this is reflected in our ecological and spiritual imbalance. Yin and Yang are a Chinese concept, but they match Shinto's emphasis on balance between material and spiritual, reason and intuition and its belief in a continuous, organic creative process operating at all levels of the universe. Musubi, the principle of creative union leading to organic growth, can be interpreted as the fusion of Yin and Yang. Yet it is distinctively Shinto in that it goes beyond such classifications, which serve only to explain or put into words the *feeling* experienced by Shinto practitioners when they make a connection with Kami.

Other Shinto shrines will freely draw upon Buddhist ideas of reincarnation – the cycle of *samsara*: birth, death and rebirth until the moment of enlightenment. This is not a part of the 'original' Shinto, but it is in many ways compatible with Shinto's belief in each life as part of the wider natural cycle, with *Dai Shizen* (Great Nature) as the source. Therefore, when an individual life ceases, it returns to nature and is recycled in a new form. Thus Shinto is capable of taking an idea widely perceived as life-denying, or at least turning away from nature, and transforming it into something life-affirming and nature centered. That flexibility is Shinto's underlying strength, which has enabled it to persist despite the arrival of continuous waves of new ideas, religious and secular, over many centuries. These ideas might have challenged Shinto, had it been a less flexible – and more abstract or ideological – faith. As it is, they have co-existed with Shinto and been influenced by it towards a greater love of nature and respect for life as it is, rather than life as some believe that it should be.

The word 'Shinto' itself derives from two Chinese characters adapted to the Japanese language. These are the ideograms 'Shin', signifying deities or the divine principle, and 'To', or Way, the same as the more familiar Chinese 'Tao' or 'Dao'. Shin is itself a Chinese translation of Kami, the Japanese word for anything connected with the divine spirit, anything that inspires a sense of the sacred or the extraordinary. Therefore we have 'the way of divine power'. The translation 'Way of the Gods' is frequent but misleading. It dates back to literal interpretations of Shinto by Christian and secular-rationalist westerners as a purely polytheistic religion consisting of many individual deities. Kami includes the concept of gods, both as beings that exist and function independently and as representations of forces within nature or the human psyche. However these beings, and the forces they represent, are linked by the underlying life force, which is the ultimate expression of Kami. And so it would be just as valid to call Shinto the 'Way of Life'. Its aim is harmonious living in which humans co-operate with each other and work with instead of against the rest of nature. That is the Way of Kami, because co-operating with nature is obedience to divine power.

Shinto is therefore more accurately rendered as *Kami no Michi*, the word *Michi* being an indigenous Japanese word for Way or Tao. A subtler, and even more authentic rendering is Kannagara no Michi, the Way *According to* Kami, the path that we find when we tune in to the divine spirit within our natural surroundings, and within our selves. Kannagara no Michi has the strongest historical resonance, because it predates the Japanese state and the imperial throne, and predates all written descriptions of Shinto. It is with this form of Shinto, its essence or inner core, with which this book is concerned, because it has produced the concepts and ways of thinking that are of most crucial relevance to our age. It is no coincidence that these are the most ancient and timeless values associated with Shinto, the most indigenous or authentic Japanese principles, which are also parts of a universal and primal human awareness.

It tells us much about Shinto that the name itself arises out of foreign influence, whereas the idea behind it is authentically Japanese and retains an inner core, a spiritual aesthetic of its own. This it does, quite contentedly, absorbing and adapting whilst remaining true to itself. In Shinto, there is no contradiction between expansion on the one hand, and universality and attachment to tradition and custom on the other. Both hands are part of the life process, the Musubi or union of continuity and change. What is now known as Shinto is a spiritual awareness that existed before the classifications and labels brought by foreign visitors and invaders, before a literate culture made it necessary to give things names, to separate, to distinguish A from B, us from them, this from that. In other words, it was the spiritual tradition of the land of Wa, before myth and fact had been sundered, before political and intellectual hierarchies became entrenched. It is no coincidence that within Shinto, the name Wa is sometimes given to a state of inner calm and peace of mind, the 'peace that passeth understanding', because it arises when the mind is cleared of concepts, categories and distinctions.

The original 'Shinto' is a faith without a name, an undifferentiated spiritual consciousness in which mind, body and spirit are continuous processes, rather than separate vessels. This faith is expressed through a way of living, Kannagara no Michi. This is a series of spiritual practices, meditations and devotions performed to honor or placate many deities, all of whom represent an aspect of our inner life. But it is also a local variant of a universal ancient knowledge, based on the intuitive leap rather than scholarly teaching or priestly authority. Shinto's value to the modern world is that it has persisted and remained essentially the same, despite adapting (or because it has adapted!) to each human epoch. In a scientific age, it reminds us of our most ancient understanding of life – a reminder we badly need, if we are to heal ourselves and shed our delusions of dominance. Rediscovering the Way of Kami could be a form of planetary Misogi, by which we begin a new cycle of living within nature, rather than trying to place ourselves outside or beyond it. It is a gentle concession of victory to Great Nature, against which we can never 'win'. It is liberation from ambitions we cannot realize and powers we do not possess, and yet it opens up new possibilities for living creatively and unlocks new powers within us.

A *Norito* in Shinto is less a prayer and more an invocation of forces within the universe that are held to be mysterious or to invoke a sense of awe. Equally, it is recognition of the divine power latent in all things and a way of connecting with that power. One such Norito has been translated as 'The Litany of the Tree' and includes the following lines:

> Trees teach us about growth
> They also stand for shelter
> They are living organisms, as water is also alive
> Ponder the meaning of growth and development
> Think of how we know nature through our senses, our eyes, our taste, our sense of smell and touch, our awareness and our deep intuitions
> ...Let us think of the trees as expressions of beauty, power, and energy united in
> endless renewal
> ...
> In the life of a tree, we may see a microcosm of the universe
> Great Trees, speak to us and teach us your wisdom
> ...
> Speak to us of the flow of life as growth and not as completion, ... as the beginning that never ends and the end that never ceases – like the acorn that grows into a mighty oak
> Speak to us of the meaning of change, purification and the communion of elements within the process of becoming eternally new.[1]

Trees have always been sacred in Shinto. Throughout Japan, there are many *shinboku*, divine or holy trees invested with the power of Kami. They are surrounded by the *shimenawa*, a thick, knotted rope that demarcates the tree as a sacred space and source of divine knowledge. There are rituals in which the specific local deity, or the more generalized Kami energy, is called upon to enter the tree. By meditating on the tree, men and women can tune into the positive influence of Kami power, absorbing it at an unconscious, wordless level. The divine energy is depicted as coming from 'above', from the 'Takama-no-hara' or High Plain of Heaven. But this also means that it comes from another dimension of the universe, another plane (as opposed to Plain) of consciousness, and from within our true selves as well. When we identify with the tree, its experience of growth and renewal, its response to the seasons and its continuous existence through the cycles of history, we understand the cosmic principle of Musubi. This is inspired by Kami and at the same time it is the animating principle behind Kami, as it is behind everything in the universe. Musubi is also represented as a deity associated specifically with sacred trees, because the tree is a symbol, and a practical illustration, of how organic growth works. In contemplating it, we understand not only the cycles of the universe, but our own processes of growth, decline and renewal. The tree is a 'microcosm of the universe' but we, in turn, are microcosms of the tree.

In our present age of environmental anxiety, we are being forced to re-learn – and quickly – that trees really are sacred, because they are the Earth's lungs, maintaining the balance that supports life. Shinto has carried that ecological insight with it from prehistory and brought it to the time when humans might need it most. In continuing to regard trees as sacred, the Way of Kami expresses an understanding of the two life processes that constantly interact throughout the universe: continuity and change, respectively the 'Yin' and the 'Yang' of the life force. These two balancing principles need each other, which is why the Norito speaks of 'endless renewal', 'the flow of life', 'the beginning that never ends and the end that never ceases'. We know that the cells in the body renew themselves continuously, but that we retain the same identity, the same essence, despite this profound change. We grow older, we lose or gain weight, our attitudes and values evolve or alter with time and experience. In other words, we become quite different, yet we remain the same.

That is the balance between continuity and change that Shinto recognizes and seeks to apply to every area of our lives. In recognition of this principle of Musubi, the Ise Shrine at Nagasaki, dedicated to the Sun Goddess, is rebuilt in identical form every twenty years.[2] Many shrines are built from wood, which is affected by natural processes and requires renewal. The principle of organic growth is reflected in the entire tradition of Shinto belief and practice. Over the centuries, it has adapted but remained constant, gladly absorbed new and external influences, shedding ideas, practices and deities that no longer seem to matter or have become obsolete. Like the shinboku itself, like the universe, like humanity, the Way of Kami is never finished, never stands still but always retains its inner essence.

The tree most sacred to Shinto practitioners, onto which Kami power is most likely to descend is called the *Sakaki* (or Cleyera Japonica). The Sakaki is an evergreen that can reach a height of ten meters, producing cream-colored flowers in early summer. In the autumn and early winter, it can produce red berries that later turn black. Thus it remains alive and awake throughout the year, but also reflects the seasonal cycles. The Sakaki is identified by the Japanese as the principal native tree, and this is another reason why it is associated with their indigenous faith tradition.

As an indigenous pathway, Shinto is on the same spectrum of faith as the traditions of the Native Americans and Australian Aborigines. It is also comparable to the spiritual paths of the Celtic and Germanic peoples, before the coming of Christianity to Northern Europe. They also experienced the sacred in trees, mountains and forests. However in the case of Shinto, there remains an unbroken thread connecting the Jomon people of 14,000-400 BCE with the urban, technological civilization of modern Japan. The Jomon produced clay humanoid or animal figures known as *Dogu*, which were seen as repositories of divine power. *Dogu* were also used as effigies for sympathetic magic and spiritual healing: the same technique that is used in some forms of Reiki treatment today. In modern Shinto, the *shintai* or 'body of Kami' can be a stone, a tree, a river or mountain, or a simple human-made object. A mirror is a popular device because it reflects the light of the sun, which is viewed as the highest divine power for the sensible reason that it is the source of all life on the planet. Swords and jewels are also frequently used, for their power and beauty make them *yorishiro*, objects that by their very nature attract sacred energy. The continuity between the *Dogu* and the shintai is evidence of Shinto's archaic roots – and its adaptability to new conditions.

From this crucial fact about Shinto, it follows that we should be careful with the word 'indigenous' and not confuse it with racial exclusivity or social stasis. Both ideas are highly misleading and dangerous. There is no such thing as racial purity and any population, even the relatively remote, contains many genetic layers. All cultures also evolve and change, even if such changes are so subtle as to be imperceptible to uninitiated outsiders. The Australian Aborigines, for example, did not simply 'stay the same' for thousands of years as incoming Europeans assumed. Instead, they responded creatively to the challenges of their environment. Their social systems and spiritual practices varied widely between regions and communities, but all of them evolved organically, and at the same time retained traditions that endured over millennia.

Movement and change have not only been constants in human history, but they are part of the natural world which humans occupy – in Shinto terms, ingredients of Musubi. Every person, indeed every life form, 'comes from somewhere else' originally. The Sakaki, sacred symbol of Japan's native faith, is equally 'native' to the Korean peninsula. Therefore the concept of 'indigenous', although powerful, cannot be completely fixed and should not be used to exclude others or assume superiority. This principle is understood by true Shinto practitioners. The modern

Japanese are not the same people as the Jomon, for since those ancient times they have absorbed an array of cultural influences from the North Asian mainland *and* the Pacific Ocean: the circumpolar region and Polynesia. It has been said that the climate of Japan mirrors this duality with is cold, Siberian-influenced winters and humid, South Pacific-influenced summers. Climate is important to the Way of Kami, because of its strong responsiveness to the seasons as expressions of the cyclical patterns of Great Nature.

Shinto is a synthesis, shaped by geography, ecology and movements of population. It is indigenous, with roots in Japanese soil as deep as the Shinboku. But like the Sakaki, it grows organically and is open to the world.

Mythology and Meaning

The names of the Kami that were born in the Plain of High Heaven [Takama-no-Hara] when the Heaven and Earth began were the Kami Master-of-the-August-Center-of-Heaven [Ame-no-mi-naka-nushi-no-kami], next the High-August-Producing-Wondrous-Kami [Taka-mi-musubi-no-kami], next the Divine-Producing-Wondrous-Kami [Kami-musubi-no-Kami]. These three Kami were all born alone, and hid their persons.

The names of the Kami that were born next from a thing that sprouted up like a reed shoot when the earth, young and like floating oil, were the Pleasant-Reed-Shoot-Prince-Elder-Kami [Umashi-ashi-kabi-hiko-ji-no-Kami], next the Heavenly-Eternally-Standing-Kami [or the Kami-Standing-Eternally-in-Heaven: Ame-no-toko-tachi-no-Kami]. These two Kami were likewise born alone, and hid their persons.

The names of the Kami that were born next were the Earthly-Eternally-Standing-Kami [or the Kami-Standing-Eternally-on-Earth: Kuni-no-toko-tachi-no-Kami], next the Luxuriant-Integrating-Master-Kami [Toyo-kumo-nu-no-Kami]. These Kami

were likewise born alone, and hid their persons.
The names of the Kami born next were the Kami Mud-Earth Lord,
next his younger sister the Mud-Earth-Lady (U-hiji-ni-no-Kami
and Su-hiji-ni-no-kami); next the Germ-Integrating-Kami, next his
younger sister the Life-Integrating-Kami [Tsunu-guhi-no-kami and
Iku-guhi-no-kami]; next the Kami Elder-of-the-Great-Place, next his
younger sister the Kami Elder-Lady-of-the-Great-Place [Oho-to-
noji-no-kami and Oho-to-no-b-no-kami]; next the Kami Perfect
Exterior [Omo-daru-no-kami: also 'perfect face' or Perfectly-
Beautiful Kami], next his younger sister the Kami Oh-Awful-Lady
[or 'venerable' lady: Aya-kashiko-n-no-kami; next the Kami the
Male-Who-Invites, next his younger sister the Kami the Female-
Who-Invites [Izana-gi-no-kami and Izana-mi-no-kami: usually
called Izanagi and Izanami].
From the Earthly-Eternally-Standing Kami down to the Kami the
Female-Who-Invites are [known as] *the Seven Divine Generations.*
Hereupon all the Heavenly Kami commanded [Izanagi and
Izanami], *ordering them to "make, consolidate, and give birth to*
this drifting land". Granting to them a heavenly jeweled spear, they
thus deigned to charge them. So the two Kami, standing upon the
Floating Bridge of heaven, pushed down the jeweled spear and
stirred with it, whereupon, when they had stirred the brine [until] *it*
became thick and glutinous and drew the spear up from the brine
that dripped from the end of the spear was piled up and became an
island. ...[3]

This dream-vision, condensed and summarized in the *Kojiki*, is
the nearest that Shinto has to a creation myth. It is not intended,
any more than a dream, to be interpreted literally and, like everything else in Shinto, it is eternally flexible. Every myth, every
story has many versions and what is important is not the myth
itself, but the *idea it conveys*. In this case, the message is one of
germination, growth and differentiation, whether between
'Heaven and Earth' (different planes of consciousness *or* areas of

the universe), male and female (expanding and contracting principle, *or* active and receptive), or even divine and human. Izanagi and Izanami are simultaneously the seventh generation of Kami deities and the primal man and woman, the ancestors of other divine principles (Kami) and the entire human race. They embody the link between divine and human: the inner Kami or the potential to become 'one' with Kami that exists in each human being is the element of Izanagi and Izanami within us.

The repetitive catalogue of names conveys a sense of the evolutionary cycle and the gradual emergence of a world we can recognize. It also calls to mind the process of awakening, slowly, from a dream, or the development of a rational consciousness that differentiates fact from fiction, the solid from the ethereal. This strange, vague myth thereby proves to be a highly efficient account of creation – the emergence of a vital principle from nothingness, an organizing principle from chaos. At the same time, it chronicles the stages of evolution: of life in the universe, of earthly geography, of levels of consciousness. The Heavenly Kami represent cosmic principles, notably the principle of growth and change (the two Musubi Kami) and continuity, or centered-ness (Ame-no-mi-naka-nushi-no-kami).The Earthly Kami represent the qualities that make life sustainable on earth, from which all life arises.

As is characteristic of Shinto, there is room for the unknown. There is no attempt to explain *why* the process started. This is because the answer is not yet known to humans: despite our scientific advances, we are really no nearer to answering the primal question of 'why' than the civilization of Jomon, or the recently centralized Japan in which the *Kojiki* was compiled. One version of the *Nihongi* touches upon the idea of a cosmic egg, an image that recurs throughout the mythological systems of humankind and acts as a point of contact between them:

Of old, Heaven and Earth were not yet separated, and the In and Yo (feminine and masculine principles) not yet divided. They formed a chaotic mass like an egg which was of obscurely defined limits and contained germs.

The purer and clearer part was thinly drawn out, and formed Heaven, while the heavier and grosser element was accomplished with difficulty.

Heaven was therefore formed first, and Earth was established subsequently.[4]

Both this account and the description in the Kojiki show an awareness that the most minuscule forms of life are the starting point for all of evolution: the 'germs' that are essential ingredients of larger or more 'advanced' life forms. The spontaneity of the development of life is captured by the phrase 'the Kami were born alone, and hid their persons'. These Kami are at once manifestations of cosmic energy and ingredients of life on Earth. They arise spontaneously from the emptiness of the universe, giving that universe shape and meaning, creating conditions in which the Earth (and other worlds) can evolve. They are the nearest in Shinto to a First Cause, because they begin the process of organic growth. When these Kami 'hide their persons', it can mean that they die off or become obsolete, replaced by other cosmic forces that continue where they left off. Kami, as part of the web of life, are subject to evolutionary change like everything else. Alternatively, it can mean that they persist as subtle influences, affecting everything within the natural cycle. The two Musubi deities, for example, animate everything in the universe, because together they embody physical and spiritual growth. The Master-of-the-August-Center-of-Heaven gives them a purpose and a sense of direction. He – or rather It[5] – acts as a point of reference for the process of growth, a place of consistency and stability. This centralizing principle acts somewhat like the base of a tree around which ivy grows, or a rock that is encrusted by moss. At the 'beginning' of Shinto, the complementary principles of stability and growth, tradition and change are clearly established.

The primal couple, Izanagi and Izanami, first created the Island of Onogoro.[6] Later, they create the islands of Japan and, by extension, the entire map of the Earth. In traditional Shinto mythology, the world is referred to in terms only of the Japanese archipelago and humanity in terms of the Japanese people alone. This reflects the 'indigenous' aspect of Shinto. It is the Japanese manifestation of a universal, nature-based faith which takes variant forms according to local conditions, including geography and culture. Looked at in this light, the Way of Kami is less racially exclusive than it might at first appear. Today's Shinto practitioner, although proud of the artistic and spiritual traditions of Japan, is likely to regard the Kannagara-no-Michi as a path for all of humanity. The ecological imperatives of Shinto give it particular relevance to the Earth as a whole, whose diverse peoples might use it to rediscover their own nature-centered spiritual paths and use them to heal the wounds inflicted on nature. Izanagi and Izanami 'invite' the whole of the planet: they are divine ancestors, but they are also our future.

Izanagi and Izanami descend to the Island of Onogoro, the first land, to have sexual intercourse and so reproduce. However, when they do this, they make mistakes and have to seek the advice of the Heavenly Kami: the significance of this event is discussed in Chapter Two below. Once corrected, they produce the islands of Japan (and by extension the entire world) and a succession of Kami deities until Izanami is burned to death giving birth to Kagu tsuchi, the Kami of Fire. In the *Nihongi*, it is said that as she lay dying, she gave birth to the Earth Goddess, Hani-yama-hime (Clay-mountain-lady) and the Water Goddess, Midzu-ha-no-me:

Upon this Kagu Tsuchi took [as his] *wife Hani-yama-hime, and they had a child named Waka-musubi* (Young-Growth). *On the crown of this Deity's head were produced the silkworm and the mulberry tree, and in her navel five kinds of grain* (hemp, millet, rice, corn, pulse).[7]

The connection between the 'five kinds of grain' and Musubi are obvious enough, as is the 'marriage' (or balance) of fire and water, two complementary principles essential to life. The silkworm denotes Chinese influence and so is a late addition to the tale, but as a gently powerful representation of Musubi it works perfectly.

Following the death of his consort, Izanagi follows her to the shadowy Land of *Yomi*. In a parallel with the Orpheus legend of the Greeks, he breaks a vow not to look at her, and so she falls away into the shadow lands, disfigured by her injuries. Izanagi is pursued, in turn, by the 'Ugly Females of Yomi' until he returns to the known world, where to rid himself of the impurities of illness and death he bathes in the sacred river Hi:

The name of the kami that was born as he thereupon washed his left august eye was the Heaven-Shining-great-August-Kami (or 'Kami-Who-Makes-the-Heavens-Shine: Amaterasu-oho-mi-kami). *The name of the Kami that was born as he washed his right august eye was His Augustness Moon-Night-Possessor* (Tsuki-yomi-no-kami, the Kami of the Moon). *The name of the Kami that was next born as he washed his august nose was His Brave-Swift-Impetuous-Male-Augustness* (Take-haya-susa-no-wo-no-mikoto,
sometimes known as the 'Raging Male', usually referred to as Susa-no-wo). ...
At this time, His Augustness the Male-Who-Invites greatly rejoiced, saying: "I, begetting child after child have at my final begetting [given miraculous birth to] *three children.* [Then], *taking off and shaking the string of jewels forming his august necklace, he*

bestowed it on the Heaven-Shining-Great-August-Kami (Amaterasu), *saying: "do thine Augustness rule the Plain-of-High-Heaven." With this charge he bestowed* [the necklace] *on her. ... Next he said to His Augustness Moon-Night-Possessor* (Tsuki-yomi): *"Do Thine Augustness rule the Dominion of the Night." Thus he charged him. Next he said to His-Brave-Impetuous-Male-Augustness* (Susa-no-wo): *"Do Thine Augustness rule the Sea-Plain."* [8]

Little more is heard to Tsuki-yomi, although moon worship continues to play a part in Shinto practice and the powers of the moon are venerated. Susa-no-wo, by contrast, became the trickster figure among the Kami deities. Through his control of the sea, he is associated with climatic variation, including unpredictable events – and including the raging torrent or Tsunami.[9] Susa-no-wo is also frequently represented as the Kami of Wind. In one Shinto legend, he becomes jealous of the supreme heavenly power of his sister, Amaterasu. He challenges her to a divinatory competition to find out which can produce the greater number of children. Susa-no-wo produces more, but Amaterasu gives birth to a greater number of males. Refusing to accept this as a victory, Susa-no-wo creates climatic and social chaos. Amaterasu goes further by retreating into the 'Heavenly Cave of Darkness' and depriving the Earth of light. As a result, crops wither and the entire life process – Musubi itself – is placed in jeopardy. Other Kami deities, sensing the threat to themselves as well as the world, gradually entice her out by placing a large mirror at the mouth of the cave. In it, she sees her beauty and light reflected and, feeling confident once again, she re-emerges. With her, the light of the sun returns and life is guaranteed. From then on, the mirror became a sacred symbol of Amaterasu, the Solar Power. Susa-no-wo is banished and comes down to Earth at Izumo, where he is still revered. Izumo, close to the headwaters of the River Hi, is the site of a major Shinto shrine, where Kuni-no-toko-tachi-no-Kami (also known as Oho-kuni-nushi-no-kami) presides. This story incorporates the legend of the deluge or climatic disruption that is common to creation myths. Therefore it also links Shinto with a universal spiritual consciousness or 'primal religion'. The rise of Amaterasu represents the restoration of cosmic order and the survival of the life force, which she embodies as a female and as a symbol of the sun. Socially, her rise represents the consolidation and centralization of power and, paradoxically, the rise of patriarchal culture: hence the number of male issue conferring victory over her brother. She also symbolizes a shift of power towards the Yamato clan, who gained a hold over Japanese life during the Nara period (710-94 CE), during which the *Kojiki* and *Nihongi* became established texts. One twentieth century Japanese account of Amaterasu describes her in the following terms:

The Sun-goddess, or the Heaven-illumining Lady, was bright and beautiful in features, unrivalled in dignity, benign, honest and meek in temper. She ruled wisely and brilliantly the realm assigned to her, giving light and life to all, and she also protected the rice-fields by constructing irrigation canals. Besides, she is represented as the organizer of religious rites, especially those in observance of the rules of purity. In short, she was the presiding deity of peace and order, of agriculture and food supply.[10]

One of Amaterasu's descendants, Jimmu Tenno became the first Emperor of Japan, the nation's legendary first lawgiver. He is also the mythical ancestor of the Yamato clan of the Nara period, from whom the imperial family descends. Amaterasu is portrayed narrowly as the ancestor of the imperial family, and hence the divine principle behind the throne. More broadly, she is presented as the ancestor of the whole Japanese and mother of their nation. But there is also a universal interpretation, more prominent today: Amaterasu as the ancestral mother of humanity and the Earth.

Where Amaterasu represents stability and order (ecologically and socially), her brother represents flux, chance and all the inconsistencies that can also be found in external nature and within all of us. At another level, he could be associated with the decentralized, less stratified and pre-literate society, free from external influences. Far from being merely an 'evil deity' (in the judgmental western sense), he represents an anarchic, spontaneous spirit that is necessary for human creativity – and evolution. And although Amaterasu is a benign force, the order she represents can become stifling and oppressive. Therefore a balance needs to be struck between the principles of Amaterasu and Susa-no-wo ('sun' and 'sea'): they complement each other in creating the conditions for human creativity and natural growth.

One Spirit, Four Souls

Shinto is a religion of life, rather than a faith that is primarily concerned with what happens after death. Instead of turning away from the world, the Way of Kami embraces it, not because it is narrowly materialistic, but because it sees our material surroundings as a gateway to the spirit. It is said that the soul is 'never lost', but recurs continuously in various aspects, throughout the cycles of time. This is not quite the same as the idea of reincarnation associated with the Indic traditions of the Hindus, Buddhists or Jains. It is associated more with the idea of organic growth and natural replenishment: the ancient cult of fertility.[11]

Thus the destiny of a soul is not determined by the actions of a specific lifetime and there is no notion of karma as a law of cause and effect. Nor is there any idea of escaping the wheel of life, as in the Indic concept of samsara. Far from wanting to 'escape' from life, the Shintoist wishes to remain within its cycle and assumes that he shall do so in some way. However, Buddhism (and with it its Indic heritage) has made deep inroads in Japanese culture and these have had a profound influence on Shinto, partly because it is such a non-dogmatic faith and partly because many people practice both religions simultaneously! Many Shinto practitioners, as we have seen, have adapted versions of karma and samsara, usually life-affirming versions grafted on to the indigenous idea of the cycle of life.

In Shinto, reincarnation is merely an aspect of Musubi, the 'endless conversions or evolutions' that make up the universe.[12] Life is held to be so important that rather than dying, a human being (or animal, or deity) will withdraw (*mi-makaru*) to reappear in another form. This intuitive sense of recurrence makes the idea of death more palatable, because it is not an 'end' in itself, but part of a larger process. However it does not claim, like some other faiths, to explain everything and there is certainly no idea of 'conquering' death, any more than there is an idea of vanquishing any aspect of nature. The element of agnosticism, of admitting that there is much we do not know about the nature of death – and hence the nature of life - is one of the most archaic features of Shinto. But it is also refreshingly modern, allowing freedom of thought and open to fresh evidence should it emerge. The sense that there is much that we do not know (whilst continuing to pursue knowledge) is part of the wider sense of humility before nature that the Shinto mentality cultivates. Awareness of the complexity and 'greatness' of nature leads to an avoidance of simple explanations, which thoughtful men and women will find hard to believe. Simultaneously, the intuitive mind is allowed to take over, and it is from this process that the idea of renewal as part of a cycle (Musubi) emerges. This is not a fixed belief or dogma, but something experienced at the level of feeling.

The idea of Musubi is rooted in the observation of nature, including human nature. It is concerned with germination, expansion, decay and transformation, the processes inherent in nature. Observing and accepting these processes is seen as a form of meditation, a way towards a spiritual appreciation of nature and, through it, the divine principle. When a human or animal corpse decomposes in the soil, it is broken down into component parts, each of which breaks down in turn and fertilizes many other life forms. From the Shinto standpoint, the same is true of the soul. Like the body, it too is broken down, each aspect surviving in its own right and contributing to new life. This is the connection between Musubi, the natural processes, and the prevalent theory of 'one spirit, four souls': Ichirei Shikon. According to Kokugakuin University, Tokyo:

*The spirit (**reikon**) of both kami and human beings is made up of one spirit and four souls. The spirit is called **naobi**, and the four souls are the turbulent (**aramitama**), the tranquil (**nigimitama**), the propitious (**sakimitama**) and the wondrous, miraculous, or salubrious (**kushimitama**). Various theories exist to explain the nature of each of the four souls and the process of the historical development of the concept. The distinctive feature of the **ichirei shikon** theory, however, is that while each of the four souls has its own particular character and function, they exist in parallel, acting together in a complementary fashion.[13]*

It is worth noting that the word 'naobi', used here, is probably related to the word *nao-hi*, meaning sun rays. These have sacred significance both because they are associated with the Sun Goddess, and because they sustain life on Earth. In early Shinto, there was a prevalent idea of Magatsuhi-no-Kami, deities responsible for all the vicissitudes of human existence, including disease, conflict and natural disaster. These were balanced by the Naobi-no-Kami ('Rectifying Kami'), born immediately afterwards, 'who remove all sin, pollution and disasters [and] restore the normal state'.[14] The idea has persisted that both humans and deities have within them a Magatsuhi-no-Kami, prone to violence and discord, and a Naobi-no-Kami, which has a moderating influence and 'leads to gentleness': this was called the

Naobi-no-mitama by eighteenth century CE Shinto theologian Motoori Norinaga.[15] In other words, violent or forceful and gentle or pacific tendencies are equal qualities within nature. They are aspects of the life process and act as countervailing forces with it. *Tama* or the more deferential *mitama* are the most common words for spirit or essential quality of any living being. In the context of Ichirei Shikon, they seem to be used more frequently than 'Naobi'. There are many words and expressions for concepts associated with the soul, which shows that the concepts are fluid and subject to adaptation or renewal.

The tama in Shinto can be identified with the western and especially Christian concept of 'soul'. To make this identification can aid understanding, but it can equally well mislead. This is why it is often translated as 'spirit'. For the tama is not seen as something *separate* from the being in which it resides, or as the pure aspect of that being. Instead, it is the essential part, the inner identity of that being. It is not destined for eternal life *outside* the natural world as much as continuity within the natural world. It is the element in each human, indeed every life form that represents the connection with nature, and connection with Kami. The Kami deities worshipped in Shinto also possess tama. According to one of Jean Herbert's informants, 'before the word Shinto was invented, the fisherman who wanted to catch a fish had to wait until the *tama* of the fish entered into him'.[16] The tama of Sakaki, bamboo and other trees is venerated. The tama is a manifestation of the Kami energy that animates all life. Anything that contains tama has the potential to become Kami.

Thus the tama is at once a symbol of individual uniqueness *and* the interconnectedness of all life. The idea that the tama has component parts and that it can divide mirrors the conception of Musubi as a synthesis or union of two or more elements, producing life in all its abundance and variety. According to one highly traditionalist interpretation of Shinto, two 'parts' of the spirit arise at different times:

The one, kuni-tama which governs the unconscious movements of the body, appears at the time of conception; the other one, wake-mitama, is really the soul of the parents, and when it arrives into the body, the soul is 'complete' and the child is born.[17]

This view of the spirit, or 'soul', displays an intuitive understanding of genetic inheritance, as well as the physical and mental development of the child within the womb. It also represents the tama, and hence the inner essence of the person or being, as a *synthesis* of two parts, one representing movement, change or flux (the unconscious bodily movements), the other stability and continuity (the parental and ancestral heritage). Without a balance of these two forces, a life form does not become a true entity: it lacks both individual characteristics and connections to the outer world.

The idea of 'two souls' is found in other spiritual traditions. In Daoism (and the Chinese folk beliefs to which it is closely related), there is a concept of *Hun-Po*, two parallel souls that move in different directions when they leave the body. The Po is associated with the physical realm. It lingers in the ambience of the body for a limited period of time – perhaps weeks or months – after the occurrence of death and then sinks into the earth from whence it came. The Hun, by contrast, ascends to the more subtle or 'heavenly' levels of consciousness. Often, Hun-Po is interpreted in terms of the Yin-Yang duality: Hun represents the abstract, reasoning Yang quality, whilst Po is the earthly, sensitive Yin. Harmonizing these two aspects of the soul is an important part of Chinese medicine, which is as interested in the spiritual malaise as the physical symptoms. Discord between them can lead to illness and ultimately death. This concept of two (or more) souls occurs in a wide range of cultures. Haitian Vodou, which is a synthesis and development of many West African traditions of great antiquity, includes the concept of two souls: the *Gros-Bon-Ange*, the individual soul or a person's 'spiritual double' and the *Ti-Bon-Ange*, which represents the individual's conscience and 'higher nature'.[18] A sense that the soul, spirit or essence of a person (or being) has more than one element, and that these elements can regain their independence, is clearly one of the most original spiritual insights of humankind.

In the Way of Kami, there are two principal 'souls', the *ara-mitama* and the *nigi-mitama*. These make up the more easily knowable aspects of the tama, the first layer of spiritual under-standing. They correspond to forces within nature and also moods, or dispositions, experienced by humans individually and collectively. The ara-mitama, or 'rough' soul, is associated with dynamic qualities, with action, with the outer world and with the power to build or tear down. The nigi-mitama, or 'smooth soul', is associated with peace, harmony, the spiritual realm and the inner life. This duality produces union, the balance of two complementary parts. Physical and psychological health depends on this balance, as does organic growth and the survival of life on Earth. An imbalance of ara and nigi mitama can produce profound spiritual ill-health, and hence physical illness. Their sundering can result in death, which is the departure of the animating principle, or essence, from the physical being.

At a subtler level, there is another pair of complementary parts, the *saki-mitama* and the *kushi-mitama*. The saki-mitama is associated with creation and life, and with these a sense of blessing (for in Shinto life has intrinsic value). It also expresses the idea of an animating power that gives life forms their distinctive features and characteristics, but also connects them to each other. *Kushi-mitama*, by contrast, signifies all that is myste-rious in the cosmos – and in the spirit, or the body, of each person or being. It stands for the unknown, the transcendent, the hidden point of origin, but also the healing power within nature.

Clues to the meanings of the four souls are found in their names. Ara is related to *aru*, meaning 'to appear to the outer world'. Nigi comes from *nigiru*, 'to consolidate the inner world'. Saki is related to *saku* ('to split, to analyze, to differentiate'), and *kushi* signifies 'to pierce, to penetrate, to centralize'.[19] These correspond, to a large extent, to the characteristics of each soul. The four souls are also referred to as *shikon* or aspects of the tama, or *reikon*. The tama is comprised of these four parts, but it is also the 'controlling spirit' to which they have subordinated themselves. In this sense, there is a correspondence between the tama and the physical body to which it gives inner life. The organs of the body are all vital to its function, and yet each organ is subordinate to the body as a whole.

The four souls all express different but complementary aspects of the human psyche, which in turn represent aspects of nature. Kushi-mitama represents the hidden dimension and so is regarded as 'beyond' the others, but also out of reach of conscious human knowledge or observation. It is the invisible within the invisible. This is why, in the *Tomoe* symbol depicting the dynamic spirit, only three principles are depicted as inter-locking waves: the ara-mitama, the nigi-mitama and the saki-mitama. The most important remains unseen: that aspect of the spirit that is mysterious and untranslatable into human terms. The Tomoe is a symbol closely associated with Musubi: three interlocking principles of growth, contraction and synthesis. Ultimately, the development of the soul is but another aspect of the principle of organic growth.

Another important feature of the tama is that it is revered after separation from the body of a person who has died. In other words, it ceases to be that person's animating principle (although it remains associated with him or her) and becomes an ancestral spirit. This, in Shinto, is at once a generalized principle of life and a spiritual guide. Revering and above all remembering ancestors is a way of preserving the continuity of the extended family group, the *Ie*. The presence of ancestral spirits in a spiritual realm parallel to our own is a source of stability and comfort. It gives to each member of the existing family group a basis of stability, a point of origin that enables them to sustain change and growth, as well as sustaining

33

them through periods of vicissitudes. Awareness of the ancestors encourages unity between members of an extended family. They are joined together in spirit even if they are geographically scattered or pursuing entirely different occupations and goals.

Revering the ancestors is, for the extended family group, a basis for Musubi: the periods of expansion and contraction that affect families as a whole, as well as each family member personally. It reinforces the idea, inherent in Shinto, that 'no man or woman is an island'. The self cannot grow or develop on its own, but acquires maturity and depth through relationships with others. In Shinto terms, 'others' include the spirits of ancestors as much as living persons. A social system based on the idea of 'autonomous' individuals competing with each other does not enable those individuals to fulfill themselves, but produces neurosis and spiritual estrangement. For the society as a whole, it generates problems such as family breakdown, addiction and violence – including violence against the environment, which results from loss of spiritual connection with nature. The ancestral tama is part of the social dimension of Musubi. It promotes a spirit of co-operation and offers a bulwark against fragmentation, enabling individuals to develop, materially and spiritually, aware that they are part of something larger than themselves.

As with all Shinto worship, the reverence shown towards the ancestral tama is concerned with aligning the spiritual and material worlds, or 'Heavenly' and 'Earthly' planes. The spirits of the ancestors are part of the Ie (extended family) and are honored at household shrines or *kamidana*. Traditionally, the role of making offerings to the kamidana has fallen upon the grand-mother of the household, although any family member can perform that function, and this increasingly happens as the generations are less likely to live under the same roof. Offerings frequently take the form of bowls of *sake* (rice wine) and sometimes small quantities of rice and vegetables. The names of known ancestors are written on paper, whilst those who are no longer known remain as a powerful background influence. The production of sake is closely associated with the idea of Musubi, which is explained in terms of fermentation (see Chapter Five). The ceremony of the kamidana is a simple observance that keeps the practitioner spiritually attuned amid the pressures of daily living. It is also a reminder that individuals and family groups do not merely 'exist' in the present, but are the product of generations of accumulated experience. Equally, the presence of the kamidana reminds the living that they too will be ancestral spirits eventually. They should therefore remember the ancestors as they wish to be remembered themselves, and should act wisely, so that they are useful guides to future generations.

'Ancestor worship' remains one of the more controversial aspects of Shinto. The use of ancestral spirits as guides is cited, by western skeptics especially, as evidence that Shinto is a 'primitive' faith without relevance to the modern world. Reverence for ancestors is one of the earliest features of Japanese spirituality, evolving generations before the term 'Shinto' arose. It is closely related to the worship of Ujigami, the 'family' or 'clan' Kami that bound traditional communities together. And paying tribute to ancestral spirits is perhaps the oldest form of religious expression, found in the ancient spiritual pathways of Africa, the Americas and Europe. Shinto has brought this form of ancestral wisdom into an urban, technological setting, where to those conditioned by western ideas of progress it might seem strangely out of place.

There is, however, another way of looking at it. Reverence for ancestors suggests an advanced intuitive understanding of genetic inheritance and the unexpected ways in which it can shape our present and future. When we realize that we are more than the products of mere chance, we can begin to fulfill our potential as human beings. Ancestors in Shinto are a reminder of the continuity of life, of biological and spiritual evolution. More than that, they connect the world of humanity with the world of Kami.

Chapter Two: Monotheism or Polytheism? And Does It Matter?

All Kami are interconnected and spring from one source – the essence of Shinto.
Grand Master Motohisa Yamakage

Eighty Myriad Kami

From a western standpoint, a question that springs readily to mind is whether Shinto is a polytheistic or monotheistic faith. Is it, in other words, a religion of many gods, associated with different aspects of nature, the universe and life experience? Or does it acknowledge only one divine principle, one source of life, one sacred power? There is also a third possibility, that Shinto is both at the same time, because a single divine entity expresses itself – or is experienced – in multiple parts.

The answer, perhaps predictably, is that Shinto is all of these things and also more. This is infuriating to those who wish to arrange and classify everything according to clearly discernible rules. But it is exhilarating to those who seek to dissolve barriers, whether between peoples and cultures or the material and spiritual dimensions. Shinto's ability to find common ground between these theological categories makes it a potential model for religious pluralism in a world community that badly needs it.

In a world of increasing spiritual hunger, the Shinto approach also offers a working model for integrating the spiritual dimension into everyday life. It shows that modernity need not bring with it the loss of soul and a compensatory obsession with materialism, which in reality fails to compensate. In the urban setting, the spiritual dimension can still be accessed as part of everyday life. It is present in business and commerce as much as in agriculture, in city streets as well as the mountains, lakes and forests of traditional Shinto observance. Paul de Leeuw, of the Japanese Dutch Shinzen Foundation, often quotes the French philosopher Roland Barthes: 'Nature is the city'. Shinto is a faith rooted in the natural world, but it accepts that the city can be as valid an expression of *human* nature as (for example) the village or nomadic encampment. All these forms of human social organization, however 'primitive' or 'sophisticated' by subjective modern standards, have the potential to become dysfunctional and unbalanced, and so destroy themselves from within. Yet they have equal potential to work with the forces of nature, as absorbed through *Kannagara*, the spiritual attunement to divine consciousness, which is the same as understanding of natural principles. Shinto practice is intended to guide men and women in this direction.

The Way of Kami accepts the city as an expression of human culture, just as it accepts that technological progress is part of human evolution. Both are celebrated as aspects of the creative power that is itself an expression of the divine energies contained within humanity. However the aim of Shinto is at once to *humanize* and *spiritualize* these phenomena. Humans are reminded that their powers have natural limits and that they should not confuse progress with the act of cutting themselves off from the rest of the natural world and pretending to be unaffected by it. For this strategy cannot succeed and has dangerous consequences for the environment, as well as social stability and mental and physical health. Therefore, the Shinto shrine in the urban setting is a gentle reminder of natural principles. Made from basic natural materials (usually wood), it is where peace and calm can be sought in the midst of activity and stress – and through that peace and calm, Kannagara is experienced. The shrine does not seek to stand out through size or ostentation. Instead, it is consciously modest and simple, a reminder of continuity amid change. The principle of the urban shrine resembles that of the sacred tree or stone within a rural

37

setting. It is a point of access by which humans communicate with the divine power, whether as an abstract force – Kami energy – or a specific deity representing a principle or an aspect of human or natural activity.

This Shinto approach contrasts simplicity with complexity, continuities within nature with the natural state of flux. It reminds us to balance the two principles and integrate them into our lives. For the Way of Kami is the way of balance. There is no divorce between matter and spirit, as there is in world-renouncing spiritual paths or 'scientific' materialism. From a Shinto perspective, an over-emphasis on the material generates neurosis and discontent. An over-emphasis on the spiritual can lead to an entrenched conservatism and social injustice, or an emphasis on rituals and traditions as ends in themselves, rather than for their inner meanings. As with continuity and change, one cannot work effectively without the other. The spiritual and material dimensions of human existence are intended to be aligned to each other and interact, whilst retaining their essential characteristics. The purpose of Shinto practice is to reinforce that alignment, both within the individual and society. How we achieve that balance is up to us. The 'us' in question are individuals, local communities, peoples and nations.

Worship is not regarded as monolithic in Shinto. It is linked to local culture and experience, as well as personal temperament or preference. Thus the reciting of Norito, silent meditation and walking in wild nature are equally valid expressions of spirituality, as indeed can be a stroll in a city park or sitting in a café. What matters is attitude and frame of mind.

In the same way, it is ultimately unimportant whether the worshipper focuses on an abstract concept of divine power or a specific deity in whom the worshipper invests certain specific qualities. Nor does it much matter how that deity is conceived. Amaterasu, the sun goddess, might for example be looked upon as the embodiment of the sun, which is the source of life. She might also be looked upon as the mother of all life, or as a representative of the feminine principle. It is possible to think of Amaterasu as a supreme deity and ultimate ancestor of the human race, or as one manifestation of a much larger divine power. Equally, it is possible to think of Amaterasu as any combination of these elements, or all of them at once. What matters is that Amaterasu provides a point of connection with the spiritual realm. In other words, it is about whether she connects the worshipper with forces outside his or her immediate consciousness. Whether the worshipper believes in the literal existence of the solar deity or regards her as a symbol of the higher power is also immaterial, as is whether she is regarded as the only deity or one among many. It is the fact of worship or meditation that is more important than analysis of the object of worship. The whole point of worship, in any case, is to move beyond analytical categories, so that the intuitive process of Kannagara can take over.

There is, nonetheless, one proviso. Amaterasu is the solar deity, the personification of the sun's power. But she is not *the same* as the sun. Amaterasu is a spiritual symbol of the sun's light and its role as the giver of life. The sun is a material manifestation of the divine power from which everything in the universe has emerged. It gives life to everything on Earth and all life forms are connected to each other by their dependence on it. When the Shintoist worships or contemplates Amaterasu, he is not worshipping the sun as such, but the life force from which it emanates. The sun and Amaterasu are parallel powers, material and spiritual aspects of the same primal power. A distinction is also drawn between the different attributes ascribed to the deity. Amaterasu as 'Solar Goddess' is distinct from Amaterasu as 'Ancestor of Humanity. They are aspects of the same deity, which is in turn an aspect of a larger spiritual energy.

We have already seen that in Shinto, Kami does not mean the same as God or gods in the sense usually understood by these words. The term encompasses the idea of an underlying power in the universe, a life force. Equally, it includes the idea of specific deities, whether as entities in themselves or as symbols of a power within nature, an emotion or an idea. And it is not necessary to 'choose' between these definitions. The whole point of Shinto practice is that there is infinite flexibility, because it is recognized that that life is complex and that different situations demand recourse to different forms of spiritual power. As we become ever more aware of the complexities of the natural world and the intricate, multi-layered nature of the universe, this approach appears more reasonable than that absolutist faiths and ideologies that polarize everything into either/or choices.

In traditional Shinto there are 'eight myriad' Kami, sometimes referred to as 'eighty myriad'. This is rarely interpreted as literally. In fact, it is rarely 'interpreted' at all by most practitioners: one of the beauties of Shinto is that it can live so well with apparent exaggeration or incongruity. Rather than an exact number, eighty myriad means an amount that cannot be quantified because it has endless flexibility and the capacity to expand or contract according to will or circumstance. Eight is a sacred number in Shinto, containing in it the connotation of infinity and associated with the life force. This shows an immense prescience or intuitive power, for we now know that it takes eight minutes for the sun's light to reach the Earth!

The presence of 'many Kami' in Shinto mythology is taken by outside observers as an indicator of polytheism. Especially confusing is the sense that deities are being worshipped as entities in their own right *and* as aspects of a universal Kami energy. Shinto practitioners seem happy with the idea that they can be both at once and the apparent lack of philosophical speculation about this question contributes to the sense that Shinto lacks system or cohesion, or that its cosmology is 'primitive' or undeveloped. Yet this acceptance that an entity can be two or more things at once and that reality has multiple parts, is one of the great strengths of the Way of Kami. Far from being backward-looking, this approach brings Shinto into line with a modern, reasoned understanding of the universe. Like other indigenous faith traditions, it is well suited to a pluralist world community and to a scientific understanding of the universe.

For Grand Master Yamakage[20], polytheism is far from a full definition of Shinto. It is 'only partially descriptive', expressing only one aspect of Shinto practice and the nature of Kami. Indeed the concept of polytheism is relevant only insofar as it contributes to our understanding of the Way of Kami as one of 'peaceful coexistence', so that 'each person's beliefs and experiences are valued'. In other words, when there are many Kami deities, or aspects of Kami energy, there are just as many perspectives on reality and there is no rigid monopoly of truth. Therefore, Yamakage concludes that:

It does not matter how one believes in and chooses to describe the divine power or powers, as long as that belief is not used to justify destructive ambitions or do evil to others.[21]

'Doing evil to others' includes all attempts to impose forms of worship, or political ideologies on others without regard for their human rights or cultural backgrounds. The spiritual quest is both an individual and a social process, but it has to evolve organically, without external coercion.

The practice of worshipping a seemingly infinite variety of Kami deities creates a culture of tolerance and acceptance. This is the case whether the worshippers approach the deities as entities in themselves or aspects of a larger entity. The expansive quality of Shinto has led to the absorption of imported Buddhist and Daoist deities. For example, the *Bosatsu* Kannon and Jizo are frequently venerated at Shinto shrines. Jizo protects those who suffer physical or emotional pain, and is also associated with children, especially those who have died and sometimes including aborted fetuses. Kannon, the goddess of mercy and compassion, also watches over children and dead souls. She is related to the Chinese deity Guan Yin, who is worshipped by both Daoists and Buddhists, and the Indian male deity Avalokiteshvara. Hachiman, the warrior god, is also worshipped at both Buddhist temples and Shinto shrines: he is the tutelary deity of the Hachiman Shrine at Kamakura, for example, and the Todaiji temple at Nara.

According to this pluralistic outlook, Kami and Bosatsu are complementary rather than in conflict or competition with each other. It contrasts with the monotheistic approach of excluding other deities or influences, and hence banishing whole areas of consciousness, thought and intuition. In the same way, Shinto is capable of absorbing ideas and thoughts from other faith traditions without compromising itself. Many Shinto practitioners are strongly influenced by ideas of karma and reincarnation that derive from Buddhism, but are no less 'Shinto' as a result. This openness to external ideas, without being threatened by them, contrasts with a distorted popular image of Shinto as a nationalistic or even xenophobic faith. It is indigenous, but capable of evolving and adapting with the society in which it arose. The Jinja Honcho (Shrine Association) welcomes 'acceptance of Buddhism, Confucianism and Yin-Yang thought' as evidence of a 'plural-value orientation'.

To sum up, Shinto might appear at first glance to be any of the following:

a) Monotheist – one divine power;
b) Polytheist – many deities or divine powers;
c) Both – many deities as an expression of one divine power;
d) Both – many deities *and* one underlying power or energy source

All this depends on from what angle that 'glance' takes place, and what cultural perspective or personal preference lies behind it. None of those four descriptions are 'wrong' in themselves, but nor do they tell the whole story on their own. We have to see Shinto as all of these definitions – and something more, that excludes definition. To connect with Kami, it is deemed necessary to empty one's mind of definitions and all forms of compartmentalized thinking. Shinto is compatible with reason and scientific thinking, as it has shown by its survival in a modern society that aspires to those principles. Yet it also complements rational thought and acts as a corrective to the excesses of pure reason, reminding us of how much remains mysterious about the universe and divine power. As Yamakage has written, the Shintoist knows that 'various kinds of mysterious phenomena occur' and 'neither excludes mystical abilities nor praises them excessively'. These abilities include those latent in humanity and those associated with divine power. Unlike those faiths that are based on certainty, Shinto seeks to remind us of how much we do not know and to celebrate that sense of mystery.

The Way of Kami combines eternal change with eternal continuity through an intrinsic pragmatism. In the same way that it absorbs influences from other faiths, it is willing continuously to increase the number of Kami deities and expand the concept of divine power or Kami energy to adapt to new situations, new knowledge and new areas of questioning. New Kami entities come into being to suit new conditions, ways of life and technologies, while ancient objects of worship adapt to new roles. The most famous example of the latter is Inari, the rice harvest deity who is now associated with business and commerce. The concept of Kami is both singular and plural ('is' and 'are'), much as the Shinto ethos of social solidarity promotes unity between 'I' and 'We'. The individual self is only fully realized through interaction with others and society is only complete when it respects the uniqueness and dignity of each individual within it. It is the same with Kami. The idea of Kami evolves organically, like the principle of Musubi that governs all growth and development (and the equally necessary contractions and regressions) within Great Nature. Musubi is likened to the process of moss growing on a rock. This is because the moss expands imperceptibly and at the same time elements of it die off or remain inert. It is one entity, yet made up of many parts. The same is true of Kami.

Types of Kami

There are an infinite variety of Kami deities and forces within Shinto. At the same time there is one underlying force which animates everything in the universe and is contained in each living being. In this context, there might seem to be little point in attempting to classify Kami deities, especially as one of the purposes of Shinto practice is to transcend all categories. Practitioners of Shinto often forget or confuse the roles of the Kami deities they revere. In general, this is not held to matter too much. If anything, it is considered to be a strength, because it contributes to the diversity and flexibility of Shinto belief and practice. But however paradoxical it might seem, Shinto practitioners do make broad – and overlapping - classifications of Kami.

For example, Yamakage refers to three classifications of Kami as portrayed in the traditional *Norito*:

1) Heavenly Kami: *Amatsukami*
2) Earthly Kami: *Kunitsukami*
3) Myriad Other Kami: *Yaoyoruzo no Kami*[22]

Heavenly and Earthly Kami can be likened to the Aesir and Vanir in ancient Norse religion. The former represent authority, order and ethics, whereas the latter represent nature's organic and spontaneously occurring processes. The Earthly Kami, like the

Vanir, are more ancient and associated with folk religion, whereas the Heavenly Kami, like the Aesir, are more closely associated with the state and, in particular, the prominence of the imperial family. Both arise from the same source: Kami energy. Therefore, unlike the Aesir and Vanir, who fought wars, the two types of Kami co-exist peacefully, fulfilling different, but equally legitimate functions.

The division between these two types of Kami, as with so much in Shinto, is blurred. It is possible for deities to have a heavenly and earthly aspect. Amaterasu, for example, is both the solar deity and the common ancestor of the human race. The two Musubi deities could be said to represent two forms of growth, vertical (Heavenly) and horizontal (Earthly). Grand Master Yamamoto speaks of two intertwined principles of 'vertical and horizontal musubi' (sic) that ensure both natural and spiritual balance. As well as natural processes, he likens them to the warp and woof in the construction of a building. Heavenly and Earthly Kami together preserve the balance between spirit and matter, freedom and order. The former include the pantheon whose activities are described in detail in the *Kojiki* and *Nihongi*. The latter can encompass ancestral spirits and local, family or community-based deities (*Ujigami*) or the expression of Kami energy in mountains, rocks, trees or any geographical feature.

'Myriad Other Kami' is an elastic term, the word 'myriad' implying the possibility of constant replication. They can include imported deities, animal spirits (such as the foxes associated with Inari) and natural phenomena that are invested with divine powers. The original meaning of *kamikaze* was the 'divine wind' that foiled a Chinese invasion of Japan. The Jinja Honcho refers to Kami of Rain and Kami of Thunder: everything 'that has a great influence on human life' can be designated Kami. The *Yaoyoruzo no Kami* can also encompass deities associated with the arts, commerce, trades and technologies – every area of human experience might be represented by an aspect of Kami.

From his extensive (or myriad?) discussions with Kannushi and their senior counterparts, the *Guji*, Jean Herbert also speaks of two loose categories of Heavenly and Earthly Kami, as described by his interviewees. He cites Susa-no-wo, the trickster deity, as the archetypal ancestor of the Earthly Kami and Amaterasu as the prototype or ancestor of the Heavenly Kami. The first is the embodiment of spontaneity and emotion, the second the personification of order, responsibility and obligation. Both characteristics are essential to human creativity and survival. The distinctions between the two categories of Kami are, however, 'elusive':

> *The best suggestion I can offer is that ... Earthly Kami are those who maintain and defend the existing status of the Earth both against further heavenly infiltration and against destructive attacks from hostile forces, while Heavenly Kami are those who endeavor to instill into the Earth further Heavenly influence.*[23]

Perhaps because of his western philosophical training, despite his immersion in the cultures of Asia, Herbert posits a more adversarial relationship between the two main types of Kami than Yamakage. But as he makes clear, he is attempting to weld together many interpretations of 'Kami nature', arising from the remarkable degree of personal autonomy enjoyed by Shinto priests. One of his Guji listed four categories of Kami, which seem to be 'more traditional' in character:

1) Physical Kami: *Tetsugaku-shin*;
2) Imported Deities: *Ban-shin*;
3) Men known to have lived on earth: *Genzai-shin*;
4) Kami of the universe: *Uchyu-shin* ('which are similar to the first category')[24]

Many Kami can fit into all four of those categories, or none of them, which demonstrates the complexity of Shinto. At the same time, it demonstrates Shinto's supreme simplicity. All of these varied ideas about the nature of Kami are valid in their own right and none of them are exclusive. They can all be seen, in themselves, as aspects of Kami energy. All that matters is that a power higher than the self is honored.

Kami Can Make Mistakes and Die

In one writing it is said:- "*The Gods of Heaven* [i.e. Heavenly Kami] *addressed Izanagi* ['Male Who Invites'] *and Izanami* [Female Who Invites], *saying: There is the country Yoyo-ashi-hara-chi-iwo-aki-no midzu-ho* [Abundant reed plain, thousand five hundred harvest], *Do ye proceed and bring it into order.'* *They then gave them the jewel-spear of Heaven. Hereupon the two Gods* [Kami] *stood on the floating bridge of Heaven, and plunging down the spear, sought for land. Then upon stirring the ocean with it, and bringing it up again, the brine which dripped from the spear-point coagulated and became an island, which was called Ono-goro-jima. The two gods descended, dwelt in the island, and erected there an eight-fathom palace. They also set up the pillar of Heaven.*"
Then the male Deity asked the female deity, saying:- "*Is there anything formed in thy body? She answered and said:- "my body has a place completely formed, and called the source of femininity."* *The male god said:-* "*My body again has a place completely formed, and called the source of masculinity. I desire to unite my source of masculinity to thy source of femininity." Having thus spoken, they prepared to go round the pillar of Heaven, and made a promise, saying: -* "*Do thou, my younger sister, go round from the left, while I will go round from the right." Having done so, they went round separately and met, when the female Deity spoke first and said: -* "*How pretty! A lovely youth!" The male deity spoke first, and said:-* "*How pretty! A lovely maiden!" Finally they became husband and wife. Their first child was the leech, whom they straightaway place*

in a reed-boat and sent adrift. Their next was the Island of Ahaji. This also was not included in the number of their children [i.e. it was considered unsatisfactory].

Wherefore they returned up again to Heaven, and fully reported the circumstances. Then the Heavenly Gods [Kami] *divined* [the answer] *by their greater* [powers of] *divination. Upon which they instructed* [Izanagi and Izanami] *saying:- "It was by reason of the woman's having spoken first; ye had best return thither again."*

Thereupon having divined a time, they went down. The two deities accordingly went again round the pillar, the male Deity from the left and the female Deity from the right. When they met, the male Deity spoke first and said:- "How pretty! A lovely maiden!" The female deity next answered and said:- "How pretty! A lovely youth!" Thereafter they dwelt together in the same palace and had children, whose names were Oho-yamato no Toyo-aki-tsu-shima, next the island of Iyo no futan-na, next the island of Tsukushi, next the triplet islands of Oki, next the island of Tsukushi, next the island of Kibi-no-ko. The country was accordingly called the Great-Eight-Island-Country." [25]

The significance of this story is not what it might tell us about male/female relationships and gender roles. However, it is drawn from the *Nihongi* of 720 CE, the 'Chronicles of Japan', compiled at a time when Japan was emerging as a centralized power with a patriarchal structure focused on the imperial court. It was also a time of profound Chinese cultural and social influences and with these came Confucian ideas stressing the importance of the male principle. Nonetheless, a strong female energy remained in Shinto to balance masculine power: the Emperor, after all, was portrayed as a direct descendent of the female solar deity. That deity, Amaterasu, is widely held to be the center of the Shinto pantheon and to represent the serene discipline of Heaven. There are a very wide variety of Kami deities in male and female form and others of indeterminate or unspecified gender. Still others, such as the Buddhist-derived Kannon cited above, can assume either male or female form. Kami energy transcends gender, but it also contains an equal balance of masculine and feminine energy – it is a synthesis of these, rather than one triumphing over another.

Needless to say, the story of Izanagi and Izanami and the pillar has been abused to justify male dominance. But when we look beneath the surface we can find a more profound meaning. The relationship of the 'Male Who Invites' and the 'Female Who Invites' to the pillar represents the complementary balance of male/female energies or (in Chinese terms) the balance of Yin and Yang. The male energy (Yang) speaks first because it is associated with outward manifestations of power: the expansive forces of the universe. The female energy (Yin) speaks second because it represents the receptive, nurturing and contracting forces. Both are vital to the creative process and ultimately it is the female who gives birth. Even during the most patriarchal phases of its history, Shinto continued to emphasize the importance of the feminine principle – through the worship of Amaterasu, as well the importance it attached to the generative process in nature and the power of intuition. Amaterasu was born from the left eye of Izanagi, and this could be said to reflect the eventual triumph of the feminine.

Gender relations, and their problems, are part of the exoteric meaning of the legend. It is at that level of consciousness that we also experience the dream-like qualities of the story, the complex catalogue of naming (characteristic of creation myths) and the phallic associations of the pillar. As in the case of a dream, we are not intended to interpret the events depicted as literally true. Although they are described in the 'Chronicles of Japan' and the 'Record of Ancient Matters', they are deemed to be pre-historic and pre-human. More than that, they are expressions of the unconscious and represent principles within nature and aspects of the creation of the universe which even a scientific age cannot fully explain through reason. The primal couple represents the transition from spirit to matter and the continuing alliance between the two principles. They are the progenitors of all life, human and non-human, and gave shape to the material universe, including the Earth. Yet they are also divine powers, expressions of Kami energy.

The esoteric meaning of the tale is that evolution takes place by trial and error and that even divine powers are capable of making mistakes. Nature – including Kami Nature – is not infallible. Nothing is 'always right', even divine powers, which is why the primal couple has to turn to other powers to help. Even those powers are not omnipotent: they cannot, for example, always prevent human beings from harming the environment and each other. Nature, as the product of Kami energy, works only when all its parts know their respective functions and co-operate with each other. When natural processes are ignored forgotten or bypassed, when human beings place themselves outside nature, there is disharmony. The inner meaning of the story of Izanami and Izanagi is many-sidedness. There is no monopoly of truth, and so spiritual evolution can take place only if we adopt a holistic and inclusive approach to life. Although one particular deity might be the object of worship, all other aspects of Kami are recognized and revered. This applies to politics, science, art and human relationships as much as to questions of faith.

As well as making mistakes, Kami can die off or become obsolete. Izanami herself is horrifically injured, decays horribly and sent to dwell in the shadowy Land of Yomi. The "Goddess of Food", one of the earliest Kami deities, is killed by a guest. Another deity named Kagu-tsuchi, was beheaded or cut into three pieces by his father, whilst Koto-shiro-nushi merely 'disappeared'. There are many other examples. Izanami 'divinely retires', Izanagi 'apparently retires', O-kuni-nushi 'becomes concealed' and Susa-no-wo 'enters the Nether-distant Land (Ne-no-kuni). According to Jean Herbert:

The Kami who thus 'die' do not thereby cease to be active on this Earth. They continue to be prayed to for blessings, and they respond. Their 'death' should therefore be taken to mean that they discarded the physical body of gross matter with which they were seen on the Earth and subsequently assumed a different body invisible to the human eye.[26]

This is a moot point. The Kami deities always existed at another level of consciousness, although they can sometimes be perceived in literal or 'gross' human form at the moment of worship, or when tales of their exploits are recounted in the form of heroic legends. However the 'death' or obsolescence of a Kami deity reflects the continuation of the human story through new phases and the evolutionary cycles of which that story is but a small part. Death or obsolescence is part of the process of organic growth, Musubi, which animates all life, including the Kami power from which life originates.

Looking Beyond the Labels

Ultimately, the terms 'monotheism' and 'polytheism' have little meaning when applied to Kami, any more than the old-fashioned translation 'Way of the Gods' helps us to understand Shinto. To understand or experience Kami we need to see beyond such labels. If we conceive of Kami as an essential unity, made up of many parts, then we are on the way to appreciating what Shinto means. This concept of unity-in-diversity, I-We, singular-plural mirrors the connections between all living organisms and also serves as a model for human behavior and the way society should be organized.

Above all, Kami remains a mysterious force and the purpose of spiritual practice is to understand it better and grow towards it. The aim of Shinto is to shine a light on that hidden world.

Chapter Three: Kami –
The Hidden World

*Whatever seemed strikingly impressive, possessed the quality of
excellence and virtue, and inspired a feeling of awe was called Kami.*
Motoori Norinaga

The Kami Dreamscape

When we dream, we are projected into a world in which the
conventional rules of gravity, shape and size, time, place and
identity no longer apply. We dream of places which are clearly
labeled in our minds – an old school, for instance, or the house
where we spent our earliest years – but which bear little or no
physical relationship to these places. Often we recognize these
differences and yet until we awake we surrender to the dream's
narrative flow. People and places routinely change dimensions.
They vanish or merge into each other. Scenes are suddenly cut or
interrupted, landscapes and colors shift before our eyes. When
we enter this world in our sleep, we are experiencing the world
of Kami whether we know it or not.

In our dreams, we experience joy, pain, fear and anger in quick
succession or at the same time. Often there is a vague sense of
awe, enchantment or foreboding. Sometimes there is outright
fear and terror. There are spectacular scenes of beauty and
passion, along with moments of quirky or surreal humor that we
cherish long after our awakening. All that is constant is the sense
of flux; all that is predictable is the absence of predictability. Even
that statement is only partially true. Sights, sounds and incidents
from years before can appear distinctly and remain frozen in
time. And dreams, as nearly all of us know, can be repetitive and
recurring. We see into the future as well as being able to reach
deep into the past or remain in an eternal present. These states of

time become artificial as they merge, interact and shade into each other. In the state of dreaming, hidden worlds within us are unlocked, unconscious desires revealed, at times explicitly, but most often in cryptic form. Through the dream world, we enter into a spiritual landscape. We are no longer bound by earthly conventions, physical constraints or material fetters. We lose our everyday 'selves', but access our true selves. Many of the actions associated with dreams, such as flying or shape-shifting – changing in form, species or identity – are also associated with the shaman's journey to parallel levels of consciousness to gain practical insights or cure psychic wounds.

Unsurprisingly, therefore, the state of dreaming is widely associated with spiritual experience and inspiration. This is true of indigenous cultures, in particular, because they appreciate the value of unconscious, intuitive forces rather than attempting to suppress them as most industrialized societies tend to do. The Aboriginal Dreamtime or Dreaming (Altjeringa) of Australia is probably the most powerful example. Ancestor spirits filled the Earth with life and shaped the landscape as they traveled across it. Having accomplished their task, they transformed themselves into animals, stars, mountains or other natural formations. They remain present in the land and just below the surface of consciousness, interacting with humans and all the animal and plant species, because they are the source of all life. The nature of Kami is not exactly the same and is part of a very different physical and cultural landscape. Yet the connection between humans and Kami follows much the same pattern.

Dreams and their interpretation also play a powerful role in Biblical and Koranic prophecy, as well as the secular science of psychoanalysis. Dreams open us to possibilities that we might otherwise ignore or deny. They allow us to conceive of parallel universes or alternative versions of reality that we cannot immediately understand. Indeed, the whole concept of understanding, analyzing or rationalizing misses the point, for that way the intuitive power (or spiritual energy) is lost. This is how dreams become portals: points of entry for us into the world of Kami and points through which Kami enter into our dimension or seep into our waking consciousness.

Chikao Fujisawa has written extensively about the connections between Shinto and depth psychology. The latter 'scientifically approaches the dimensional depths of the psyche for the purpose of recuperating the dynamic unity of faith and reason'.[27] As a spiritual science, Shinto starts from the premise that there is no 'gulf' between faith and reason, but they are on a continuum. This is because it 'has never lost its primal contact with the sustaining dimension of the depths of life, from which all special beliefs must have emerged in the past'.[28]

Shinto, in other words, has preserved its intimacy with the world of dreams, or the spirit world, and at the same time embraced all the characteristics of reason and modernity. It has never divided ancient and modern, faith and reason, conscious and unconscious, dream and reality into opposing camps. Nor has it erected barriers between them, so that 'modernized' men and women lose contact with the archetypal images and insights that bind us together as humans, connecting us with Great Nature and the cosmos. Such loss is ultimately a loss of self, or in shamanic terms *soul-loss*. In Shinto, by contrast, the most ancient archetypes and primal dream images are joyfully celebrated and made relevant to an urban, technological society based on the exercise of reason. This process of integration is not consciously orchestrated. There no reason why it should need to be 'thought out' because the natural flow of consciousness between humanity and nature has not been interrupted. There is no need to 'reconcile' the conscious and unconscious areas of the mind because in Shinto practice they influence (literally *'flow into'*) each other continuously. The interaction between them corresponds to – indeed is part of – the interaction between humanity and Kami.

Depth psychology, meanwhile, is a process of reconnection between modern men and women and the archetypes or, as Carl Gustav Jung calls them, 'primordial images' that underlie human behavior and actions. These archetypes can be seen as the starting points for the evolution of thought, before an artificial division was inserted between imagination and ideas. Equally, they may be viewed as the beginning of humanity's spiritual evolution. As such, they remain part of our intellectual and spiritual DNA, running parallel to our genetic inheritance. They are expressed in our mythologies, legends and folk tales and children's stories. They also form the basis of the great religious and spiritual traditions of humankind. We experience them at a personal level, which defines at our individual level, but also as part of the *collective unconscious*, a shared human experience that binds us to our fellow human beings: in Shinto terms, a Musubi or union.

Jung cites as a prime example of archetypal consciousness his dream of a phallic deity. This primordial image also appears as an image of Kami in popular Shinto. Its celebration in a sophisti-cated urban context looks incongruous to most westerners, but not to the Japanese. That sense of incongruity is itself the reason why depth psychology has emerged in the west. For it arises out of a sense of loss, because a mechanistic worldview has confused rational-ism as an ideology with reason itself.[29] As a result, western humanity has been disconnected from its real nature and true instincts. Its flow of consciousness has been disrupted by the pursuit of 'pure' reason at the expense of our imaginative and intuitive powers, which are at the heart of our spiritual being. To the Shinto practitioner, imagination and intuition come from the Kami power within us, which to our great detriment we have buried.

The civilization that has separated conscious and uncon-scious, imagination from idea has produced much that is of lasting value in the sciences and creative arts especially. Yet the suppression of archetypal energies is now catching up with us and is the origin of the crisis affecting western society at many different levels. Western civilization's collective blind spot about intuitive and unconscious forces has undermined and even destroyed many of our finest achievements. Isolated from intuition, reason has turned against itself so that intelligence that should be used creatively and productively has been diverted towards destructive ends. Nuclear and other 'weapons of mass destruction' are the most potent (indeed archetypal!) symptoms of this malfunction. But the effects pervade a culture that has come to exalt aggression and competition over co-operation and fellowship. At the individual level, this aggression is increasingly directed against the self: addiction to alcohol or drugs, self-harm, anxiety and depression are expressions of spiritual longing and disconnection from the inner self.

Such aggression is a natural response to the stifling of the flow of consciousness (Kannagara in Shinto) that connects humans to each other and to the rest of nature, including its spiritual aspect. It is reflected in consumerism, with its aggressive pursuit of material things as ends in themselves, in the growth of violence, family and community breakdown within western societies and societies influenced by the west. Closely related to these symptoms are aggressive and exploitative relationships with non-western peoples and the one-dimensional ideologies that equate relentless economic expansion with 'growth', whatever the human or ecological cost. And it is also the separation of humans from their archetypal consciousness that fuels the ecological crisis and the dangers it presents to all of life, including our own. Archetypes are often in animal form or human-animal hybrids. This reminds us of the continuity between humans and other species and hence of our position within the natural world. If we lose that sense, then however much we learn about the Earth or the universe, we have lost the sense of connectedness between all areas of life.

Depth psychology has emerged as a means of healing western consciousness. It stems from a desire to reunite the many parts of that consciousness that have been hewn apart and placed in opposition to each other. More than that, it is a way of reconnecting with unconscious – or spiritual – energies, the suppression of which has resulted in individual neurosis, social dysfunction and a destructive relationship with our environment. In western civilization, there is a rich tradition of connecting with primordial images. The cave paintings of Lascaux, in south-west France, express the connections between man and nature through both the hunting and the worship of animals. This is natural cycle familiar to many indigenous cultures even today. The Inuit, for example, worship and revere the animals they hunt, because they are the source of life.

The indigenous religions of Europe reflected the same understanding of our intimate connection with nature, which is why interest in them is reviving at a time of heightened ecological awareness. Like Shinto, they experienced the sacred in trees, mountains, rocks and streams. The idea of archetypes was explored extensively by Plato and was expressed in the most of the religious practices of ancient Greece and Rome. The use of icons as instruments of meditation and prayer, by the Orthodox Churches in particular, is also an expression of archetypal consciousness. Icons are human archetypes, points of entry to the dimension of the spirit. Therefore the process of healing advocated by depth psychology is reuniting western culture with its true self, just as it reunites individual clients with their inner selves. A vital part of this process is the rediscovery of a sense of enchantment, the 'awe' spoken of by Motoori. It transcends language and conceptual thought, but it is the basis of all lasting and worthwhile human values. This primordial sensibility is found in the world of dreams and is identical with reverence for Kami.

Shinto practice is also about bringing together the disparate areas of human consciousness into a whole. But in Shinto, they have not been forcibly separated or sundered, but constantly interact and overlap. Depth psychology can use the world of dreams, or conscious exercises in visualization, as a way to access primordial images, so that the parts of the human psyche can be brought together. It is a form of psychological Musubi, a re-binding of the different parts of the self to produce something more complete. Although depth psychology has emerged from a secular, rationalist culture, it reaches beyond that culture. And, as Jung and many others have realized, its logical conclusion is spiritual development. The emergence of therapies that recognize the importance of the world of dream (or Dreamtime) and acknowledge the world of the spirit demonstrates the relevance of Shinto to the west at this stage in our cultural development. At a time when we are questioning our social and ecological priorities, especially a narrow and materialistic idea of 'progress', the Way of Kami shows us that we can keep (and increase) our scientific knowledge and our reason *and* at the same time connect with nature and the world of the spirit: the hidden world of Kami.

In Shinto, the starting point is the intuitive power of the mind and its relationship to the spiritual dimension. Archetypes are more than mere creations of the mind. They are representations of something that exists outside as much as within the human psyche. The primordial images are therefore images of Kami power. That power is the animating principle of the universe, uniting (as in dreams) past, present and future, conscious and unconscious, matter and spirit. Shinto practice begins with an acceptance that products of the human imagination that put us in touch with that higher world are in themselves real. It therefore does not matter whether specific deities 'exist' or not, or whether the myths and legends that surround them are 'literally true'. Such arguments miss the point because they come from the restrictive either/or logic that stands in the way of spiritual development. More important than the archetypal images in themselves is the power or essence that they express, and which we use them to reach.

The shamanic practitioner and writer Serge Kahili King expresses well the difference between western psychological and indigenous spiritual approaches to consciousness when he contrasts the therapist's work with images to the shaman's journey to different dimensions or 'worlds':

> These are dream-worlds in which symbols **are** reality, inextricably linked to outer reality, in which interactions with the symbols **are** interactions with their counterparts in the outer world. This is an area in which more and more modern therapists are becoming involved [through] "creative visualization" and "guided imagery". [They] acknowledge the effectiveness of working with symbolic imagery, but I doubt whether many would acknowledge [the images'] intrinsic reality.[30]

Serge King works with Huna, the Hawaiian system of sacred knowledge that has many aspects in common with folk Shinto. Throughout Polynesia, the concept of *Mana* (or *Tiki*) as an all-pervasive life force closely resembles the idea of Kami energy. The Kannushi in Shinto absorbs some of the functions of both therapist and shaman. He acts as a conductor of Kami energy, but also enables us to find that energy within ourselves. The Kannushi helps us, as individuals, to connect to our primordial or dream images and integrate them in our waking lives. At the same time, he enables us collectively – as practitioners - to align ourselves with Kami power. He is a human instrument of Musubi: the union, or tying of a knot, between material and spiritual realms, or expressed another way, the union of Earth and Heaven.

The landscape of dreams can be used to illustrate the relationship between Kami and humanity. This, in turn, helps us to experience the spiritual system of Shinto, the Way of Kami. In dreams, the dead are routinely resurrected. We find ourselves in contact with relatives (whether we wish to see them or not), with friends (or enemies) former colleagues or teachers, neighbors, companion animals (such as dogs or cats) who have 'passed to the other side'. This powerful popular phrase in English, with equivalents in other western languages, corresponds directly to Shinto thought. The other side is another state of consciousness that remains accessible to us and can guide us, if we are attuned enough to Kami energy.

The presence of the dead, as guides or advisers, or reminders of suppressed emotions, helps us to understand the role of ancestors in Shinto practice. They are our psychological and genetic heritage and so they influence us now and in the future – and they affect our descendants as well. Through dreams, we reassemble our past selves and project ourselves into the future. Equally, Shinto is based on the sense of continuity within change, and change within continuity. The three 'worlds' of past, present and future are not separate but overlapping and revolving together. They are at once governed by Kami itself and also by specific aspects of Kami.

In the shape-shifting quality of dreams, we can also sense what Kami is – or are. For Kami is singular and are plural simultaneously: much as in many traditional Japanese communities the terms 'I' and 'We' become blurred or interchangeable. Kami *are* individual deities, spirits or archetypes which are worshipped, revered or placated in their own right. At the same time, Kami is the principle of animating energy or pure consciousness, on which the universe was founded and which connects all forms and aspects of life. Kami is an external force, but it is also within each of us. It gives us individual life, but defines as part of collective humanity and, more than that, an integral part of Great Nature.

Through Kami, we stay in touch with our most ancient understanding of humanity's place within nature. We sense the power of natural forces, a benign power when we work with it, threatening when we arrogantly defy it. We feel the spiritual presence immanent in everything around us. Yet through Kami, we encounter the most advanced scientific thinking that interprets the reality in terms of waves that flow and fluctuate, sees ecological linkages and psychic 'resonance' between living systems and sees the universe as a series of connected parts or 'folds' that overlap, so that nothing can be said to be *entirely* autonomous or separate.[31]

Through reason, we are arriving at a holistic understanding of the cosmos that matches Shinto's appreciation of Kami energy as the pervasive force. The new world of sub-atomic particles and dark matter corresponds with the ancient world of Kami, based on the intuition that there are many levels of reality and consciousness coexisting and balancing each other. We access Kami at the points where spirituality and the new science appear to intersect: the strange and seemingly inexplicable sensations of déjà vu that are part of every human experience; the power of coincidence or *synchronicity* to affect every area of our lives, and the 'chaotic' association of apparently random events or phenomena into an intricate pattern.

All this, in Shinto terms, is Kami. There is a real possibility that a cycle of human understanding is coming full circle, with our intuitive and rational faculties reunited. In the Way of Kami, they never were apart. The beauty of Shinto is that there is no need to reconcile the singular with the plural aspects of Kami. They are distinct and they are simultaneously the same. Kami who are individually revered might represent any aspect of the universe. These can include human activities like writing, painting or commerce, or a natural phenomenon like rain, snow, wind and sunshine. Yet just as all these distinctive elements of the universe are connected, so each Kami worshipped in his, her or its own right is a part of the whole Kami energy that connects all life together. And in worshipping an external Kami deity, or a representation of Kami in a stone, stream or sacred tree, we are reaching for the Kami within ourselves. The sheer diversity of Kami, and the fact that all are part of the same essences, creates a spiritual system of inherent flexibility and pluralism, in which religions and deities that spring from different soils are given equal status as manifestations of Kami. According to Fujisawa:

> *Therefrom derives the proverbial tolerance of Shinto, which willingly admits co-existence with other faiths.*[32]

When we contemplate Kami, our principal aim need not be to understand what it is, or what they are. In place of understanding, we need to enter into the spirit of Kami, to 'go with the flow', or Kannagara, rather than over-analyzing and so putting up barriers. Entering the world of Kami means entering a dreamscape in which we leave all our preconceptions behind to assume nothing – and everything.

An Infinite Variety

> *The Japanese mind in all ages has been quite content without definite conceptions of Kami. The people have not cared to idolize Kami, even to their spiritual sight.*
> Tasuku Harada

There are so many types, varieties, subsets and archetypal images of Kami that it would be easy to become confused and sidetracked and so miss the essence of Kami. This is a classic case of 'not seeing the wood for the trees', for in the pursuit of elusive details and classifications, the student risks losing the true meaning of Kami. That true meaning, if it can be adequately summarized in words, is the veneration and celebration of life in all its manifold aspects. Here, Shinto contrasts most clearly with those religious traditions of both east and west that emphasize withdrawal from the world and self-denial, and which at their worst create climates of fear, prohibition and punishment. In Shinto, spiritual practice is equated with affirmation rather than denial, positive engagement with the world rather than withdrawal from it. This does not in any sense imply uncritical acceptance of the world as it is, or the pursuit of material above spiritual ends, or condoning exploitation of humans or the violation of nature. Such behavior is held to be anti-life, denoting estrangement from Kami. For Shinto practitioners, engagement with the world means working for a just and equitably balanced society, the wise stewardship of natural resources and the conservation of the environment, on which we depend for life itself. Forests, for example, are sacred, as is each tree within them. They are repositories of Kami, and they are also the Earth's lungs.

According to the *Kojiki*, there are 'eighty myriad' Kami. We have seen above that we need not take this number literally, for it is intended to imply an unquantifiable number that has the possibility of limitless expansion. There are Kami to represent all aspects and permutations of the natural world, all human activities and all areas of the human psyche. These Kami are themselves aspects of an all-encompassing Kami energy. Like all energy, Kami can neither be created nor destroyed. However it can expand and unfold into new aspects and functions. Simultaneously, it can contract as some of its aspects fall into disuse or are superseded, in keeping with evolution and human progress. Kami therefore follows the rules of Musubi, organic growth and continuous change balanced by underlying continuities. And yet Musubi is a product of Kami energy and is represented by two, or sometimes many more, Kami deities. When we accept this apparent paradox, we are well on the way to experiencing the essence of Kami.

Therefore it can be said that there are Kami for every

occasion, and every occasion is an expression of Kami. Kami archetypes can disappear, merge with each other, divide into two or more, evolve, or change shape, form, gender and character.[33] They can also die or be killed. When this happens, it signifies changes in the natural world or human society. The Kami do not literally die (archetypes or deities cannot, after all), but return to the primal energy source and re-emerge in new forms. In all these activities, the Kami powers follow patterns found in the rest of nature. For Kami is (and are) a part of nature, and nature contains and reflects Kami. Yet Kami is also the creative power from which the universe, the Earth and all natural phenomena arise. To use a suitable western term, it is the 'First Cause', and as such is external to us, or situated on a 'Heavenly Plane'.

However Kami also remains within us, around us, accessible to us when we tune into it through natural or man-made objects. In Shinto practice, there are two parallel worlds or planes of consciousness, that of Kami and that of humankind. But they are not only parallel: they overlap and shade into each other. Shinto practice aims to bring the two planes of consciousness into alignment (Musubi). Thereby, the 'hard power' of human intelligence and energy is modified by the 'soft power' of subtle Kami energy that flows through everything in the universe, connecting us to fellow human beings and everything else within Great Nature.

It follows that strictly defining Kami, either in singular or plural form, is a difficult and arguably pointless task. As a force that is eternally shifting and evolving – whilst remaining eternally constant – Kami are inherently difficult to 'pin down'. To do so is counter-productive, because it interferes with the flow of life that Kami both generates and represents. To use a highly suitable English colloquialism, the definition of Kami is *as long as a piece of string*. Therefore any definitions should be seen less as conclusive 'facts' and more as guides or pointers towards a larger understanding or feeling. Jean Herbert provides a list of possible attributes of Kami which he does not claim to be absolute or definitive. For how could it be, when Kami is by its very nature a flexible, elastic and inclusive force, reflecting all the riches of nature and humanity? It is worth reproducing Herbert's list here, in an edited form, because it illustrates two aspects of the question. First, it shows the complex array of meanings and associations that Kami can have, and the problems that can arise from chasing definitions rather than feeling and experiencing Kami's true meaning. Secondly, it illustrates the psychological and ecological insights subtly contained in Shinto thought, gained by attuning to the spirit of nature.

Definitions and Descriptions of Kami

1) A specific word meaning 'which possesses a superior power';
2) A provincial pronunciation for the word *kimi*, master, lord;
3) A mispronunciation of the word *yomi* or *yomei*, Hades;
4) A derivation from the Ainu word *kamui*, 'he who (or that which) covers or overshadows';
5) A derivation from *kamosu*, to brew or ferment;
6) A derivation from *kabimoye*, to grow and germinate;
7) A modified form of *kabi*, mould or fungus;
8) An abbreviation for *kagami* (or *kangami*), mirror. According to Ansai Yamazaki (seventeenth century) because 'the heart of the [*sic*] Kami is pure like a clear mirror, without a single trace of dimness'. Or according to K. Tanigawa (eighteenth century) because *kagami* means *kagayaite-mieru*, 'to appear bright or brilliant'.
9) An abbreviation of *akami*, the All-seeing, meaning literally *akiraja-ni-niru*, to see clearly;
10) An abbreviation for *kan-gami*, 'shining-see'. According to M. Imibe because 'the Divine mind, like a clear mirror, reflects all things of Nature, operating with impartial justice and not tolerating a single spot of uncleanness';
11) An abbreviation for *kakushi-mi*, [that] 'which hides itself';

12) An abbreviation for *kakuri-mi* or *kakure-mi*, a hidden person, a hidden body.

13) An abbreviation for *kagemi*, shadow-body;

14) An abbreviation for *kashi-komi*, fear, awe, reverence.

15) A combination of *ka*, 'which relates to something hidden or dim like the shadow and the fragrance of a flower *(kaori)*', and *mi*, 'which relates to something visible or tangible, like the fruit, the flesh and the body, all called *mi*.' This view, which is held by various modern scholars, was already defended by Hidenari Hori (nineteenth century) when he wrote; 'The *ka* sound has the sense of hidden, mysterious, invisible and intangible ..., while the *mi* sound represents fullness or maturity. ... So the word *Kami* means something of nature, invisible and intangible';

16) A combination of *ka*, strange, and *mi*, person. Therefore a person 'possessed of mysterious or marvelous substance';

17) 'A subtle combination of fire *(ka)* which blazes up vertically, and water *(mi)*, which flows horizontally';

18) A combination of *ka* (a demonstrative prefix) and *mi*, which stands for *hi*, the Sun.[34]

These interpretations of Kami were distilled by Herbert over three decades of research and visits to Japan (1935-1964). There are many others he discovered, such as kami [sic] denoting hair, the top of the head and head-waters.[35] These were not deemed significant enough to be included in the central (but non-definitive) list of nineteen attributes. But they convey much about the true nature of Kami, especially to the student of Shinto in the decades since Herbert, who is likely to be drawn in particular to its ecological and organic aspects. Hair grows – and recedes – organically, its development linked to a wide variety of shifts and changes within the body. From one strand of hair, a person's DNA can be extracted and so their identity and genetic inheritance is exposed. Much can also be learned about that person's diet, health and general sense of balance with nature.

The top of the head represents purity of spirit in many cultural traditions, including Shinto. In Ayurvedic medicine and in many forms of Reiki, it is the Crown Chakra which is the seat of pure consciousness and a portal for divine inspiration. It represents the summit of human potential, including the potential for alignment with Kami, and corresponds to the summits of mountains which possess sacred qualities. The head-water is a center of energy, a place of striking natural power and beauty. There, two currents of water meet and each one *becomes* the other. This dramatizes for us the relationship between Kami and humans, spirit and matter, the union or synthesis (Musubi) by which two forms of power connect and transform.

A large part of Herbert's research consisted of long talks with Kannushi, Guji and Grand Masters. He also read extensively the works of academic historians and theologians of Shinto, some of them his contemporaries but many from previous centuries. The term *theologian* is used by Herbert presumably on grounds of convenience and convention, but reflects only one facet of the truth. The 'theologian' of Kami is part-poet, part-scholar, part-philosopher and part-seer. He[36] is not a theologian in the conventional or literal senses. Kami is not God, although it could be said to include, and transcend, a concept akin to an omnipotent creator. Herbert cites, for example, the fifteenth century CE founder of the Yoshida Shinto sect:

The Kami appeared before Heaven and Earth of which He was the Creator. He forms and surpasses the positive and the negative. He is the Kami in Heaven and on Earth; the spirit in all creation; and the soul in humanity. The soul is the Kami. Therefore the Kami is the source of Heaven and Earth; the spiritual nature of all Creation; and the destiny of humanity. The Kami is immaterial, and yet gives life to the material.[37]

The 'He' is metaphorical, denoting the creative aspect of Kami energy and also Kami as first principle or 'source'.[38] At first glance, the language is reminiscent of Judeo-Christian or Islamic conceptions of God – and hence the relationship between God and humanity. The Creative Kami is the giver of life and the Supreme Being. A closer reading reveals a profoundly different view of creation. From the Shinto perspective, creation is not a single event or series of events, but a continuous, unfolding process. Nor does it have a beginning or an end. Instead it is a recurring cycle of organic growth animated by cosmic energy. This is why Yoshida's words are expressed in the present tense. Shinto is the Way of the Eternal Present[39], in which all points in time are brought together, which is why it is also the Way of the Ancestors. The life-force passes through constant cycles of growth, contraction and transformation. This is expressed a general principle of life, a universal Musubi, on which all Shinto beliefs (and evolutionary theories) are based. Kami is – and are – regarded as the 'deification of the life force' which, as Fujisawa says, 'pervades all beings animate and inanimate'[40]:

Kami is the invisible power which united spirit and matter into a dynamic whole, while it gives birth to all things without exception.[41]

Through an appreciation of nature and respect for our fellow beings, we become attuned to that invisible power. Through the workings of nature, and human societies that work in harmony with nature, the invisible power makes itself known to us. Therefore we experience Kami through an acceptance of the evolutionary and generative process of Musubi: organic growth and the union between spirit and matter. Many of the definitions and descriptions of Kami gleaned by Jean Herbert refer to the principle of Musubi. There are references to brewing and fermenting, which correspond to one of the meanings of the word *musu*, as well as representing the whole process of organic change. This is no coincidence. The Shinto mentality draws no distinction between simple natural or human actions (the 'micro') and the broad canvas of humanity or nature (the 'big picture' or 'macro'). One is an aspect of the other. Both need each other. Therefore the most profound understanding of the divine power is expressed, and explained, through the most routine human or natural actions.

Germination and growth are also mentioned, as is mould or fungus, for what better or simpler illustration could there be of organic growth, the seasonal cycle and the cycle of all life? This is equally true of fruits and flesh, which decay and return to the earth to be replaced by new life. The sun, without which there could be no life, epitomizes Kami, and so is revered both as a deity and as an empowering principle. A symbiotic relationship between Kami energy (divine but accessible) and Musubi (material but subtle) is made by the Jinja Honcho, this relationship being itself a form of Musubi or fusion of divine and earthly energies:

> *The natural life power which gave birth to things was called Musubi (divine power of growth) and this divine musubi (sic) – namely a divine nature and power – was perceived in the manifold workings and phenomena of nature.*[42]

The Kannushi interviewed by Herbert display a typically pragmatic approach to their faith. This is viewed as evidence of their level understanding and commitment, rather than a sign of weak faith and worldliness, as it might seem to the western mindset. The Kannushi is at once a spiritual guide and a craftsman. He is concerned principally with 'what works', rather than abstruse theories that can easily seem remote and so create barriers to spiritual development. His strength comes from a primal awareness of Kami. From this comes the ability to tune in to Kami energy and convey it to others. The Kannushi works with Kami as a living reality, not an abstract theory or an absent, remote being. In this context, Kami energy is the equivalent of the sculptor's metal, wood, or clay, *and* the tools with which he turns them into works of art.

Like a sculptor or painter, the Kannushi conveys images that give others insights into themselves, but also link them with something higher than the self. In this instance, it is the flow of Kami power. The Kannushi can work with an array of archetypal images of deities to bring to life the idea of Kami, or more correctly specific aspects of Kami. He can use modern images appropriate to an urban society, abstract images that express sensations and ideas simultaneously. Or he can use images that combine old and new. For example, there can be few more effective illustrations of the Musubi principle than the blades of grass that seem to arise spontaneously from cracks in the pavements within mega-cities like Tokyo, New York or London. The product of seeds wafted from afar, they should remind urban men and women of their origins and spiritual roots.

In general, Shinto Kannushi make use of tried and tested images that connect modern humanity with the ancient past, but remain relevant to us today. Brewing, for instance, is an ancient and valued craft in Japan as much as it is in Europe. Kannushi work with images of Kami that reflect intricate and fundamental natural processes in an intelligible way that can be observed through the seasons, or through the process of living, growing and maturity. Thus there are many images of ripening fruits, which also recur seasonally, and images such as hair that reflect stages in the life cycle. Kannushi continue the tradition of presenting Kami as individual deities with human or sometimes animal characteristics, with whom we identify as individuals when we access the power or wisdom they embody.

This leads us inexorably towards the question of whether these individualized Kami are deities worshipped in a 'literal' sense as higher beings. Or should they merely be seen as metaphors for generic human or animal characteristics, powers or desires? Once again, the answer eludes the classifications and definitions characteristic of western logic. To illustrate the problem, here are two definitions of Kami cited by Herbert that initially appear to contradict each other. The first is from Naofusa Hirai, published in 1960:

> *The Kami are not merely abstract beings, but are individually endowed with divinity and respond to real prayer.*[43]

The second was provided by Banzan Kumazawa in 1940:

> *The Kami have no form, but only function. On the contrary man has both form and action. The Gods cannot surpass the actions which have form, and men cannot surpass the wonderful functions that have no form.*[44]

From a western perspective, one of these propositions must be true, the other false. In Shinto, however, both viewpoints co-exist. More than that, they are both true simultaneously. At the act of worship, they assume the archetypal form of human or animal. That archetypal image contains, for the worshipper, the essence of Kami. The aspect of Kami energy that is the object of worship, contemplation or entreaty is connected to all other aspects of Kami energy: it is one facet, or fold, of the whole. In this way, the worshipper of Amaterasu is worshipping an individual deity who represents the qualities associated with motherhood and nurturing, qualities associated, in temperate climates at least, with the sun's benign rays. Less directly, the worshipper is contemplating his or her origins, with Amaterasu standing for the primal mother of the human race, the supreme ancestor who began our evolutionary cycle. Beneath those layers, the life-giving role of light is implicitly understood and affirmed and with it the power of the sun as the origin of the life cycle and all organic growth. That leads in turn to an understanding of Kami as the underlying power within the universe. Amaterasu can be worshipped as the supreme solar goddess and mother of life, or as the essence of the sun, or as the idea of everything that is good and life-affirming in nature. Whichever way, the spiritual and scientific forms of knowledge meet in her and are bound together.[45]

The same process is replicated in worship of all Kami deities, as aspects of universal Kami power. Kami deities therefore 'are' and 'are not' entities in their own right, just as in traditional Shinto ethics 'I' and 'We' are the same. They illustrate the relationships between the individual human and human society, and thence the human species and the rest of nature. Concepts of 'divine' and 'deity' are not ends in themselves, but aspect of a larger life force that connects everything. When Kami worshipped as individual deities, each one has certain specific powers or influences (shintoku), derived from his or her own 'lofty authority' (mi-itsu). Yet these powers can sometimes be shared between many deities (or aspects of the same deity). As with radio waves, the signals sent out by Kami powers can vary in frequency and strength – from the Ujigami who act as guardians of small communities or extended families to the Kami worshipped at open shrines as guardians of the Japanese people and by extension the whole of humanity.

Kami deities are neither all-knowing nor all-powerful. They make mistakes, learn and develop, or sometimes fail to do so because of inherent psychological flaws.[46] Izanagi and Izanami, the first couple who are the progenitors of humankind, initially produce 'inadequate' offspring who do not have the necessary creative energies (see Chapter 2). They ask for and accept instruction from more senior Kami. Susa-no-wo is noted for his petulance, childish outbursts and the characteristics of the Trickster, which is why he is associated with winds and storms.

They are also characteristics that are part of the human psyche, which lead to mistakes but can also be harnessed for positive ends. Kami represent the range of emotional experience and can act as outlets for emotions that are played down and suppressed for the common good.

And Kami, as we have witnessed above, can also die out and be replaced. Herbert cites in particular the case of Izanami, the female member of the 'first couple', about whose 'decomposition and putrefaction' there are many 'lurid details'.[47] These represent an aspect of Musubi: decomposition and transformation, which are crucial to the process of organic growth. Also, there are the cases of Kagu-tsuchi, beheaded or cut into three by his own father; the Food Goddess, who is murdered by an angry guest. Another Kami, Ame-waka-hiko is killed by an arrow and Kotoshi-nushi 'disappeared'. Susa-no-wo 'enters the Nether Distant Land (Neo-ne-kuni) and O-kuni-nushi merely 'becomes concealed'.[48] The mirror is a recurring symbol of Kami energy and power, and the world of Kami mirrors the world inhabited by humanity. By experiencing Kami, we see ourselves reflected as if in a mirror, but we also cross into a parallel universe or dream-world, which is in fact a higher plane of reality.

We can therefore see that there are a seemingly infinite variety of definitions of Kami, many of them overlapping, most of them multi-layered. Jean Herbert bravely distils them into the following:

An entity invisible to the human eye in our normal state of consciousness, capable of exerting an influence on our visible universe, and to which worship should be offered.[49]

This is as exhaustive a definition as it is possible to arrive at, except that it does not differentiate between Kami as deities or archetypes and Kami as universal energy. But, as Herbert knew, the whole point of Kami is, ultimately, its elusive nature. It is (or they are!) a force that transcends concepts and language. Motoori's list of characteristics expresses the spirit of Kami because it is at once eclectic, comprehensive and cautious. He lists:

- *All the gods of Heaven and Earth and their mitama* (spirits)
- *Humans, birds, animals*
- *Plants, trees, seas, mountains*
- *'Anything that has an extraordinary or eminent character'*
- *'The entities that have to be feared'*
- *Emperors*
- *Tohotsu-kami ('Distant Deities')*
- *Thunder*
- *Dragons*
- *Tengu (mythological figure)*
- *Foxes*
- *Peaches*
- *Rocks*
- *Tree-trunks*
- *Leaves*[50]

Some items on this list have become obsolete since Motoori's day. Few modern Shinto practitioners are likely to believe in dragons although the dragon could still be a symbol of latent power. The notable feature of the list is its empirical quality, the sense that it can be added to at will, according to the practitioner's situation and experience. It is far from exhaustive. Indeed the assumption is that it should not be, but should include and absorb as required. Like the list of characteristics complied by Herbert, they emphasize the idea that all that is alive contains Kami, and offers access to Kami. They recognize categories of life: human or animal, plant and mineral are all part of nature's web, as are geographical features. Through each of them we can see an element of the divine.

Cycles of life and seasons are acknowledged through fruits that ripen and leaves that shoot and later fall. Their colors and textures change as they pass through the cycle of life and once they die off they regenerate. These simple natural processes provide a working model for how the rest of the universe works and so enable us to understand and approach Kami. Mythical beings balance that understanding because they remind us that there is much about the universe that we still do not know, therefore we must preserve our sense of humility. 'Distant Deities' have the same effect. They also remind us of the hidden depths of the human psyche, the forces within us that we cannot express verbally or classify in a rational way. Tree trunks have roots that reach deep in the soil, reminding us of our own ancestral roots and the continuities within nature, of which we are part. Weather patterns such as thunder make us aware of nature's elemental power and how we, as humans, are ultimately subordinate to it, however socially and technologically advanced we might be come. This is a salutary lesson for our present age.

Motoori's list also includes Emperors and by extension 'the entities that have to be feared', whether human or divine. They grey area between the two types of authority was acknowledged by traditional Shinto. Political power was held to derive from Kami, but that brought with it the responsibility to exercise it justly and in keeping with Kannagara-no-Michi.[51] All authority is ultimately spiritual, whether it is the power of rulers and politicians, the elemental power of nature or our own inner discipline. Those who exercise power are bound by a contract that includes Kami as well as those over whom that power is exercised. Ruling means interpreting and understanding natural law – the Kannagara – and making sure that its patterns are replicated in human society. The basis of that spiritual authority is interdependence and co-operation.

This approach contrasts with the over-powerful state and over-dependent population, characteristic of totalitarian regimes (of 'left' and 'right'). But it contrasts equally with the exaggerated individualism of some western societies, expressed especially in 'neo-liberal' economics. Under this system it is claimed that individuals and the 'choices' they make are sovereign, but in reality arbitrary and uncontrolled 'market forces' take precedence over individual and collective interests alike. The underlying problem is a failure to understand that markets, and economics itself, make sense only when they serve the interests of communities and take account of culture and ecology as much as measurable statistics of profit and growth. The individualism of this form of economics (and the political ideology associated with it) is too narrow to be psychologically or spiritually satisfying. It encourages a distorted relationship between human beings, in which they are isolated from each other or locked into sterile competition. From this follows a distorted relationship between humanity and the environment, in which the latter is considered separate and hostile, but ripe for exploitation and 'conquest'.

In reality, human beings are far more than simply consumers of natural resources. We 'look after ourselves' by looking after each other. Our truly rational interests match our intuitions and spiritual sensibility rather than economic statistics, therefore the wise stewardship and preservation of our environment – cooperation with nature – is the best way to ensure quality of life and human survival. In Shinto terms, the over-mighty state and the over-mighty market both disrupt the balance of Kami energy. This is why their environmental and human consequences are, in the end, the same.

Such imbalances are created when the 'feeling of awe' is lost. Fear (in the context of 'those entities that have to be feared') does not mean abject terror but a sense of reverence and wonder, an understanding that there are powerful forces that should not be disrupted or polluted by human activity. The feeling of awe expresses an aesthetic sensibility at the heart of Shinto. It is a reverence for all that is beautiful in the natural world, as an expression of the beneficent power of Kami. This appreciation of beauty in that which is simple and close to nature is reflected in Shinto shrines and objects of worship, as well as being the guiding force for Japanese art and design through the ages.

In Shinto practice, a distinction is drawn between Kami itself and the object of worship or reverence that denotes Kami: 'between [the deity or aspect of Kami] and the material object in which it is believed to reside, whether a tree or a mountain or a stroke of lightning or the mirror in the innermost [shrine] sanctuary'.[52] The object is not *the same as* the Kami deity or that is being worshipped. However its *essence* contains that Kami. And that Kami is linked to the universal or collective Kami, the source of life. We are therefore looking at three layers of consciousness:

- The object, natural or human-made, through which Kami worship takes place
- The Kami deity, or archetype, representing a human or natural quality, an aspiration or desire, a people or place, etc.,
- The universal Kami energy, of which the Kami deity is an aspect

To take one example, the deity Takami-Musubi-no-Kami is known as the 'High Tree Deity'. He is often represented by a sacred tree (*himorogi*) encircled by a sacred enclosure (*iwasaka*). Himorogi means 'sacred tree' and 'tree of life' at the same time, as the concepts are interchangeable.[53] Takami-Musubi-no-Kami is one of the Musubi deities, a means by which the principle of organic growth is recognized. This principle, as we know, is an aspect of Kami and the main means by which Kami energy is disseminated. Thus the sacred tree is an embodiment of organic growth. The enclosure then makes it a point of meditation through which the sacred power of growth is accessed in the image of Takami-Musubi-no-Kami. That image in turn provides access to universal Kami energy.[54]

Often, the worshipper is not consciously thinking about these layers of consciousness, which as with so much in Shinto overlap anyway. The worshipper is quite likely to lump all three layers together and this in itself will do nothing to obstruct his appreciation of Kami. Alternatively, he or she might focus on one aspect, seeing the tree (for instance) as the expression of organic growth and through that accessing the specific and universal aspects of Kami it represents. Ultimately, it does not matter as long as a deeper understanding of Kami is arrived at and the worshipper is more committed to Kannagara. The whole point is to move beyond verbal reasoning and beyond categories.

Equally, Shinto practitioners frequently 'forget' or 'confuse' Kami deities. This happens in exactly the same way as we forget the names of people, or confuse one person with someone else whom they seem to resemble. In the case of Kami, the underlying energy is the same. Therefore, confusing the various aspects of Kami at once 'matters' and 'does not matter'. It matters in the sense that knowledge can, for many, be an aid to spiritual development. Deities or archetypes such as Takami-Musubi-no-Kami offer links with the history of Shinto as an ancestral tradition passed down through the generations, constantly evolving and changing to suit social changes, but retaining its essence. In another sense, they increase our understanding of forces within the human psyche, or the workings of nature in which we are embedded. They are tools of personal growth and ecological awareness that point towards the origin and essence of life. The presence of Kami deities reinforces the tolerance and celebration of variety that distinguishes Shinto from absolutist religions and gives it an especially potent message today.

Yet it also does not matter because an excessive dwelling on detail can be both confusing and obstructive. The essence of Shinto is intuition. Each individual Kami is, as we have seen, an aspect of collective Kami. It is also a 'primordial image', the point at which the individual unconscious meets the collective unconscious. For a practitioner of Shinto, what matters is the experience of Kami, rather than precisely *how* Kami is experienced or what area of Kami energy is invoked. The Kami deity is part-guide, part-instrument of the spiritual awareness which is the original Shinto.

We can therefore return to the earlier analogy with the painter or sculptor. The Shinto practitioner (and more especially the Kannushi) is akin to an abstract artist who studies and works with classical forms before deciding to transcend them. The classical education is a process of grounding. It provides a framework of knowledge and an inspiration for experiment and discovery. In Shinto forgetting or overlooking details and distinctions is often a sign of spiritual confidence and maturity.

The Idea of Kami

I do not know what exactly is here, but feeling some gratitude I cannot help crying.

Saigyo[55]

The Buddhist monk Saigyo (Sato Norikiyo, 1118 – 1190 CE) retained a love of and tenderness towards nature and his meditation took the form of living for long periods on remote mountains. He saw the sacred in the natural world and his 'crying' represents that sensibility. Like so many aspects of Japanese Buddhism, and Japanese spirituality more generally, this is a continuation of the Shinto tradition. Shinto has, in the same way, been influenced by Buddhism, Daoism and other belief systems, willingly incorporating their ideas and imagery. It is a spirituality of inclusiveness, which is capable of looking outwards to expand its vision of the world and looking inwards to renew itself. It can change and simultaneously retain its central core. It has no dogma or doctrine that can be imposed on others, but it is *felt* and experienced by its practitioners and those who fall under its spell.

Kami is – and Kami are – the psychic power behind Shinto and the life energy of the universe. We come into contact with Kami when we acknowledge the sacred in 'steep mountains, deep valleys, forests [and] landscapes'[56], in cities and parks, and most of all within ourselves. Acknowledging the sacred means seeing beneath the surface, the overt characteristics, into the essence of a human, an animal, a natural formation – anything we choose to turn into a point of contact with the divine. When we do this, we are also able to look more deeply inside ourselves and see beyond the petty ambitions, feelings of anger and resentment and warped priorities that form like layers of dust and dirt on a clear glass surface. Seeing the sacred in nature, or rather *behind* nature, is the way we access our inner Kami. The natural world holds up a mirror into our soul: when we pollute nature, we are polluting ourselves; when our lives are based on conflict and greed, we find only ugliness in the world around us. Connecting with Kami makes us 'cry' with wonder and enjoyment, as well as 'gratitude' for being alive. It is a process of spiritual cleansing, through which we rediscover what is essential in ourselves.

Connecting with Kami is therefore the opposite of withdrawal from the world. When we look inside ourselves, we do not abandon the world but seek renewed inspiration to improve it. We are reminded that we *are* each other and also that the natural world is an extension of us, and we of it. Kami is one and are many. Awareness of Kami means that we are become aware of our true individuality, which derives from our connections with the environment and our fellow beings. Kami power connects us with everything in the universe. It gives us a sense of proportion and perspective on life. Yet it also makes us aware of our potential as human beings. It makes us part of something larger than ourselves that links us to the earliest forms of life, but is still evolving and transforming itself.

Kami is the hidden power that takes us beneath the obvious but in so doing elevates us. The idea of Kami is to move beyond the world of ideas, concepts and facts and letting the power of the intuitive imagination take over. In Shinto, it is this constantly renewed act of surrender that is the basis for ethical conduct, which means finding the Way of Kami. The process of looking for and then following that path is known to Shinto practitioners as *Kannagara no Michi*.

Chapter Four: Kannagara – Going With the Flow

The person who is on the **Kannagara-no-Michi** *should naturally be both an artist and a moral man.*

Jean Herbert

'All Is Well – All Is Perfect'[57]

Kannagara is less a set of beliefs, more an attitude or disposition. It is less about moral judgment in the orthodox sense and more about aesthetic sensibility. It is more about acceptance than questioning, intuition than idea. Kannagara lies at the heart of Shinto, as a mentality, way of life and spiritual practice. Sometimes the very term Kannagara is used to differentiate Shinto as a coherent whole from a varied spectrum of folk customs and beliefs. And yet Kannagara is so nebulous, so lacking in clear shape or content, that the question arises of whether it is a philosophy at all.

By asking that question, we miss the whole point of Kannagara. If we demand that it provide 'answers', we make the same mistake as critics of abstract art who condemn its lack of recognizable form and claim that it doesn't 'look like anything'. Like abstract art, Kannagara is the expression of unconscious forces. Yet it is also a way of seeing reality more clearly, reaching beneath layers of false consciousness. Kannagara takes us beyond conventional questions and criticisms, beyond the conscious search for answers, beyond words and concepts as we usually understand them. It asks us not to challenge, not even to question, but to yield and in so doing acquire a subtle – and supple – form of strength.

Kannagara-no-Michi is an alternative and in some ways more expressive rendering of the name 'Shinto'. Michi means Way or spiritual path, in the same sense as the 'To' in Shinto and the Chinese Tao or Dao. A man or woman of Michi is one who has a sense of natural justice and a social conscience, who lives a principled, simple life and has achieved a state of inner calm. As Tasuku Harada writes:

> A man of Michi is a man of character, of justice, of principle, of conviction, obedient to the nature of his humanity.[58]

Michi is consciousness of our true nature, taking us beyond superficial, transient attachments or desires. The principle and conviction spoken of by Harada do not imply dogma or an inflexible mentality – these, after all, denote attachment – but an understanding of the true self and the true state of things, and therefore the true priorities in life. The 'man of Michi' is not suggestible nor swayed by passing fashions or fads, nor given over to given over to consumerism. One who is conscious of Michi is aware of the destructive consequences of such delusions. He or she retains an inner core of integrity arrived at by calm reflection and meditation, by attunement to the spiritual power of nature, from which all life flows.

Kannagara is a subtle concept, meaning 'attunement to Kami' or 'in accordance with Kami'. Kannagara-no-Michi can therefore be interpreted as 'the Way in accordance with Kami' or 'the Way of attunement to Kami'. Through Kannagara consciousness, we unite the spiritual and temporal words. For, in the words of one of the Kannushi interviewed by Jean Herbert, it is 'repugnant to separate what is above from what is below'.[59]

In other words, there is no division between what we have learned to call 'spiritual' and what we have learned to call 'material'. They are different levels of reality and Kannagara is the means by which we bring them back together. By so doing, we acquire a better understanding of our selves, our world and our universe.

Thus Kannagara expresses the intuitive complement to scientific reason, the spiritual counterpart to technological advancement, the often Yin energy that softens and in a literal sense *humanizes* the Yang. But is also expresses the Yang energy that is essential for creativity and life. Michi, like the Tao with which westerners are more familiar, contains both hard and soft powers, the 'conviction' and the 'obedience', the masculine and feminine principles, the constant interplay of which sustains the whole of nature. Kannagara leads us towards Michi, the state of balanced energies. When we know and experience Michi, we see what is really there, rather than what we have been conditioned to wish for.

Kannagara leads us towards a sense that 'all is well – all is perfect' within the universe. Nature is a benign order in which everything is connected, rather than a series of disconnected parts in perpetual competition, as we have tended to believe in the west. Moreover nature is not something hostile or 'other' from which we should separate ourselves and put up barriers against. When we do this, it leads to personal and collective neurosis, individual and social disintegration. We are turning away from Kannagara and so we are turning away from ourselves – and from Kami. Nature and Kami are identical: when we realize our true nature, we access the Kami power latent in each one of us. In Shinto, we are all potential Kami, much as in Kabbalah the divine spark continues to burn with us all.

And so Kannagara-no-Michi is also the 'Way of Kami Consciousness'. It asks us to use our intuitive skills, the right side of our brain, the ability to sense and feel as well as reason and think. We are offered a way back to nature and a way to connect with the universal life energy that connects us to all other beings. Kami Consciousness is 'the awful daring of a moment's surrender', to borrow a powerful phrase from T.S. Eliot's seminal poem *The Waste Land* (1922). That is to say, it is the ability to draw back from our immediate concerns, our material entanglements, and see that we are part of something much larger than ourselves, that we are part of the common endeavor that is life itself. We realize our true selves not by asserting and demanding, but by co-operating and yielding, seeing ourselves as part of a cycle of life, not standing outside it or superior to it. Kannagara is a sense of perspective, through which we see, or lightly feel, the invisible strands that connect all living things and all ecosystems together.

Perfection is glimpsed by us when we cease to struggle for it externally. When we cease to care about having the perfect society, the perfect home, the perfect body, we see the qualities of perfection in nature, humanity and our inner selves. 'Perfect' societies turn into dictatorships and collapse. 'Perfect' homes are sterile and characterless. 'Perfect' bodies succumb to illness or eating disorders and, like all other bodies, eventually die. The pursuit of pseudo-perfection is quite literally a dead-end and it blinds us to all that is positive in life.

This approach is reflected in the Japanese aesthetic of *Wabi Sabi*, which sees perfection in (for example) sculptures or ceramics that are rough hewn or unfinished and thereby closest to nature. Wabi Sabi teaches us to see perfect natural beauty in a rainy landscape or storm-tossed coastline as much as in the 'perfect' sunrise or sunset. Nature's perfection is expressed through flaws, through asymmetry, through the raw and unfinished – unfinished because the natural cycle is never complete. When we try to 'finish' it, when we falsely identify perfection with rigidity, we disrupt the flow of energy that is Kannagara. As Sensei (Aikido Master) William Gleason explains it:

> **Kannagara** is the flow of nature, the seasons of the year, and the unfolding of human destiny. It is the evolution of the universe as both matter and consciousness. There is no absolute beginning. This feeling is celebrated in Japan's annual festivals. The new year in Japan honors the past and prepares for the future.[60]

Surrendering to Kannagara is going with the flow of nature and the universe instead of trying to overpower it, which both reason and intuition tell us can never work. Here the traditional image of King Canute trying to turn back the tide can help us understand. The unstoppable waves are Kannagara and the king standing by the shore represents the human (and especially western) delusion of dominance and command over natural forces, in other words the pursuit of pseudo-perfection. Another very effective way of translating Kannagara-no-Michi might be 'The Way of Going With The Flow of Kami'.

Kannagara is about the peeling away of illusion and release from shallow materialistic goals. But in dispelling delusions of grandeur, it unlocks access to a flow of energy that pervades all that is alive and connects all living systems together. We become aware that there really is 'more in heaven and earth' than is dreamed of in materialist or narrowly individualistic philosophies – or in that false 'humanism' that is used to justify the rape of nature in the interests of artificial 'growth'. Through such philosophies, the inner self is contracted and we lose touch with the powers we possess. Kannagara expands the self and so we become aware of new and more significant powers. They are not really new, of course, but as old as the universe, powers to which supposedly 'primitive' peoples access all the time because they experience nature more directly and with fewer illusions of dominance.

The science of Reiki is more directly influenced by Japanese Buddhism than Shinto. However, as we have already observed, Kami Consciousness has interacted creatively with the Buddhist dharma for many generations. In effect, they are two intertwined spiritual ecosystems that depend on each other, feed off each other and grow together. Reiki is the 'universal life energy' that is used as a healing power by the Master or practitioner. That energy must be tuned into and worked with through a process of surrender to the flow of that energy. We do not 'harness' or 'capture' it because that will not work. Instead we give in to it, let it flow through us, become aware of ourselves as instruments of universal life energy.

Students of Reiki undergo a process of attunement. This can also be seen as a practice of Kannagara-no-Michi. It is about learning to yield to the energy of life rather than trying to control or suppress it, as we do in so much of mundane living. The life energy is an expression of Kami and its ultimate source, according to Shinto tradition, would be Amaterasu, the sun goddess who represents the origin and sustenance of all life. Recent scientific thinking, such as the awareness that much of the universe is made up of dark matter (and speculation about parallel universes) are also expressions of Kannagara. They are areas where reason and intuition, science and spirit meet. For both the scientific and the spiritual quests involve being able to envisage things outside everyday consciousness: to make the journey to Upper and Lower Worlds. They are about seeing connections that are usually hidden from view. As a science and as a social movement, ecology makes explicit the connections between living systems that nature-centered spirituality under-stands by intuition.

Far from abandoning technology and renouncing scientific knowledge, we should learn to use these gifts in balanced and skilful ways. That is the next stage of social evolution and Kannagara follows the evolutionary flow rather than obstructing it. Non-technological peoples and indigenous cultures might have a greater affinity with natural processes than most supposedly modern men and women. But through awareness of Kami, we rediscover that connection. We learn to use our knowledge in a different way, in tune with *Dai Shizen*: Great Nature.

Realignment with Great Nature

Dai Shizen is the vast cosmic setting into which we are born, where we live and within which our lives find any meaning.
Grand Master Yamamoto Yukitaka, Tsubaki Shrine

Through Kannagara, we are able to develop a moral sensibility that is aligned with natural forces. We discover a system of ethics derived from nature. This approach contrasts with most conventional understandings of morality. These have tended to place human morality well outside or 'beyond' natural instincts. They have also tended to use ethics as a means to distinguish human from non-human, humanity from nature. In western thought, whether Christian or humanist in flavor, there has been a bias against nature as something violent, threatening and malevolent, beautiful only when 'tamed' and controlled. Perhaps the clearest example of this way of thinking is the seventeenth century English philosopher Thomas Hobbes, who wrote that the State of Nature creates a 'war of every man against every man', in which life is 'solitary and poor, nasty, brutish and short'.

Nature, then, is something to be hidden from, fought against and where possible overpowered. But it also represents a constant danger, both externally (in the form of floods, disease and earthquake, for instance) and within the human psyche as the dark, natural forces that are a threat to civilized values. This makes the education and socialization of young people into a process of de-naturing, the denial of threatening natural impulses in order to build 'character'. It becomes the instilling of narrow forms of knowledge and the placing of limits on the imagination.

The corollary of this approach is that nature is something to be held in contempt and treated as ripe for exploitation. What is feared at one level is also viewed as an infinite resource to be dominated and trampled upon. The use of naked power to bind other species, notably through factory farming and vivisection, is justified by secular myths of human superiority and automatic human precedence. The burning of rain forest to make way for cattle ranches and the mining of sacred mountains are justified in terms of progress and growth, without reference to anything other than immediate human gratification. The more 'things' we *extract* from nature and the further from natural processes we seem to live, the greater the quality of our lives is held to be. This is why the environment is sacrificed to human consumption and nature is marginalized by orthodox economists.

According to this view of nature as enemy of progress, peoples who live closer to nature are less advanced than 'us'. Therefore, it follows that they and their cultures are expendable. There is a direct parallel between the 'conquest' of the North American and Australian landscapes, for example, and the attempt to destroy Native American and Aboriginal societies. Such 'conquests' are never fully successful, and attempts to control the environment have many unintended consequences, such as desertification. In Australia, for example, Aboriginal wisdom is offering useful insights to an urbanized population struggling with prolonged drought. The increasing appeal to indigenous lore and understanding of the land is accompanied by a cultural and artistic revival – and an increasingly effective political movement to go with it.

In the United States and Canada, increasing interest in Native American spirituality among both native and non-native popula-tions is part of a growing environmental consciousness and also a spiritual awakening. It stems from awareness that, in drawing up boundaries against the natural world and defining progress in narrow human terms, something important has been lost. By elevating the human over everything else, we have paradoxically lost sight of what it is to be truly human, truly alive.

The conventional western view of nature is hierarchical, with technological man at the top. The hierarchy is conceived of in terms of steps upwards or rungs on a ladder. Often it is depicted as a pyramid, significantly a human-made structure. Indigenous peoples, animals and plants are arranged below humankind in order of levels of 'advancement', with the most (apparently) elementary organisms at the bottom. Within the human realms, technological societies occupy the highest echelons, agrarian and hunter-gatherer societies the lowest. There is a hierarchy of religions as well, with monotheism at the top and below them the nature-centered spiritual paths, which acknowledge many deities or multiple expressions of divine power. Such beliefs and the societies that nurture them are inherently less 'advanced' and enlightened. John Stuart Mill, the great nineteenth century liberal thinker, made it clear that his theories of individual freedom did not apply to those peoples 'still in a state of nonage' (meaning infancy or immaturity): a reference to Africans and Asians under European colonial rule.

This hierarchy of nature and human cultures is a secular humanist version of a more traditional Judeo-Christian vision of a 'Chain of Being'. Yet in the Chain of Being, God is placed above humanity and there is a common thread that links all living beings: they are a part of God's creation. The Chain of Being therefore engenders a certain degree of humility in man, in contrast to the secular, enlightened or 'progressive' mentality that is essentially mechanistic. It seeks to deny or sanitize the spiritual, accepts the existence only of gross matter and stresses separation rather than unity.

Humanity and nature are therefore viewed as separate and opposed, as are masculine and feminine, mind and body, reason and intuition, tradition and progress. And humans themselves are separate from each other, locked in competition for personal advancement and access to resources. Thus it is the denial of nature, rather than the State of Nature, that gives rise to a war of all against all. The denial of nature is also a denial of the spiritual dimension, which is in turn a denial of underlying unity. And so the quest for knowledge and objective truth that fashioned the European Enlightenment mutated into a narrowing of consciousness and an expansive vision of human potential contracted into a mean vision of human isolation. The narrow version of the Enlightenment world view is rapidly becoming old-fashioned, overtaken by mounting ecological concerns and increasing social fragmentation. These phenomena are leading an increasing number of western men and women to question the mechanistic ideology of progress and the materialistic values of the consumer culture. They embark on a quest for forms of spirituality that that they can use to make their lives more complete. Scientific reason is itself debunking all or most of the assumptions behind mechanistic and linear thinking. It is finding connections between all living systems. In the process, it is discovering that organisms once thought elementary and hence unimportant (plankton, for example) can play a critical role in maintaining the Earth's equilibrium. This subverts the 'step-ladder' or pyramidal view of nature and shows that human life depends on a balance between living systems, something that 'primitive' peoples – and practitioners of Shinto – knew all along.

However it would be unfair, and contrary to the spirit of Shinto, to present the mechanistic world view as the only expression of western consciousness or even inevitably the dominant one. Most people in the west love the natural world and feel as intimately connected to it as peoples elsewhere. And it is in the west more than anywhere else that the modern environmental movement has taken shape, because people there are increasingly aware of the spiritual and ecological costs of development. Finding the presence of the divine in natural formations has roots as deep in European cultures as in Japanese or Native American. One of the first acts of Christian mission-aries to the Germanic peoples was the cutting down of sacred trees. This symbolized an approach to development that has stayed with us, to our detriment. But within Christianity there is as strong a respect for nature as in any other faith. Love for all of God's creation is an integral part of Christian belief and western ecologists – religious and secular – look to Saint Francis of Assisi as one of their pioneers because of his love for the natural world and emphasis on animal welfare. Monastic orders such as the Franciscans are enjoined to live simply and close to nature, eschewing consumerism. Indeed the destruction of the environment has coincided with growing secularization and the decline in religious observance, just as rising concern about the environment coincides with a revival of interest in spirituality.

Similarly, it would be unfair to dismiss all of the Enlightenment tradition as mechanistic and anti-nature. From the eighteenth century onwards, much of the western Enlightenment was about arriving at a better understanding of how natural processes worked and influenced human society. It was about greater pluralism and tolerance, questioning received wisdom and coming to terms with new and unfamiliar belief systems. Enlightened thought retained, indeed strengthened, the notion that nature could be modified or tamed, but held in common with Shinto the idea that nature could, and should, be worked with and accommodated. The problem with the Enlightenment has been the way its legacy has been distorted, taking only its emphasis on abstract, detached reason and melding it with political and economic ideologies that see nothing other than the grossly material. Both the 'right' and 'left' polarities of western-style politics are committed to different versions of the same materialistic vision.

The Romantic Movement grew out of the Enlightenment, although it reacted strongly against the emphasis on 'pure' reason. Romanticism enshrined nature in the arts and restored a sense of awe and wonder. It countered the idea that 'man is the measure of all things' with a sense that, in Blaise Pascal's words, 'the heart has reasons that reason does not understand'. It raised the status of the authentic and the primitive over the manufactured and planned. The Romantics believed in intuition, that 'Beauty is Truth, Truth Beauty, That is All' .[61] This belief is virtually identical to the Shinto consciousness of Kannagara and continues to exert a powerful hold over the western imagination today.

Therefore, there is no necessary East/West division and there is no incompatibility between nature-consciousness (Kannagara) and western thought processes. There is much evidence that we in the west are groping our way back towards our own version of Kannagara. As well as environmentalism, this is expressed through such movements as Creation Spirituality within the Christian churches - and the revival of interest in Kabbalah in Judaism and Sufism in Islam. It is expressed through the attempt to reconstruct ancient Pagan pathways from the fragments scattered by history. Science is taking us back to our original awareness of our continuity with nature. A more inclusive idea of 'rights' is beginning to encompass other species, and the ecosystems that determine our survival. This is why Shinto is so profoundly relevant. Without pleading, lecturing or demanding, it shows us that we can reconcile our modernity with following the path of Great Nature, through changing our attitude rather than abandoning what we know. The example of Shinto can guide us back towards a western Kannagara.

The focus on the west should not be allowed to obscure the equal problems of the East. Or, to put it a better way, the estrangement of humankind from nature is a global problem. East Asian societies (including Japan, but in recent decades China and India especially) have rushed to embrace western models of development, with their confusion of short-term gain with long-term welfare and their insistence that only material possessions can provide fulfillment. They have assumed that the alternative to poverty has to be consumer society. In making that assumption, these societies have generated both ecological and spiritual crises within one generation. Material wealth has increased, but so has inequality and relative poverty. Many people have more 'things', but there is also pollution of the atmosphere and poisoning of water supplies. Rapid urbanization has led, on an accelerated scale, to many of the problems that have become familiar in the west: family breakdown, violent crime including domestic violence, alcoholism, drug addiction and the array of mental and physical illnesses that affect western men and women. Worst of all these addictions is addiction to consumerism itself.

Dislocation from the land that sustained them and the communities that nurtured them have left millions of people alienated from the spiritual practices that only made sense in the context of nature's rhythms. So disturbed by these developments have the Chinese Communist authorities become that they have renounced militant atheism and are promoting spiritual values, albeit within strict parameters. Confucian principles are valued especially, because they emphasize duty and obedience as well as personal responsibility, although Daoist and Buddhist temples and monasteries have also received state support and the spread of Christianity is tolerated. Concern for the nation's spiritual ecology is mirrored by growing anxiety about the natural environment and the effects of chronic water shortage and atmospheric pollution. Across the 'developing' world, the wisdom and ultimate effectiveness of western-style development are beginning to be questioned, much as they are in the west where they originated. There is a sense of inner as well as outer desertification, of spiritual as well as environmental pollution. There is also a longing to reconnect with nature and with the practices and rituals that have made sense over generations. This type of spiritual cleansing is one of the motifs of Shinto.

Within eastern spiritual teachings, there is also a strong tendency towards renouncing the world, which is also a turning away from nature. There is a danger at times that transcending the world takes precedence over living at peace with it. Shinto and other indigenous traditions (such as Tibetan Bon) act as a countervailing force, reminding the spiritual practitioner of the value of life, friendship, love, a sense of beauty in nature and within the human person.

Yet in east and west alike, the old-fashioned, essentially nineteenth century view of progress still exerts a remarkable hold, especially in the economic and political spheres. These remain almost wholly locked into mechanistic models based on continuous economic expansion and 'growth' and on the false assumption that natural resources are infinite – physical law. They assume that humans have the automatic right to extract as much as possible from nature, without humility or any sense of the need to co-operate fellow humans, let alone other beings. One reason is that the continuous growth model creates political and economic elites that become attached to their privileges. Attachment is the central problem, because the pursuit of material gains is transformed into an end in itself. Human relationships and human responsibilities towards the natural world are subordinated to this material quest. Since most of the gains involved are transient, a state of perpetual restlessness and discontent continues to affect us.

The present growth-based economy has become the principal cause of unhappiness and neurosis, because the growth is not organic, but unbalanced and dislocated. This, in turn, creates a culture of fear: fear of death, because the idea of a continuous cycle of life has been lost; fear of nature, because its 'wildness' gives the lie to human invulnerability and separateness, and fear of fellow humans, because the growth-based economy trans-forms them into competitors for material resources. Above all, we are induced to fear our inner selves, the spirit (or Kami energy) within that is telling us that something is wrong with the values that influence our personal and collective behavior. Thus the external and internal problems of our civilization arise from the same source. Environmental and social breakdown and spiritual-psychological crisis are symptoms of our disconnection from Kannagara.

Our sense of loss, created by distance from Kannagara, is often experienced at an inarticulate, unconscious level. It is the cry of revolt, against the reduced and diminished self as much as any dehumanizing (but human made) 'system'. This is why so much aggression is turned inwards, through addiction and self-harm. The dislocated relationship with nature is replicated in dislocated relationships between human beings. The numerous social and psychological problems experienced by 'developed' societies (and increasingly replicated by the developing world) are indicators of profound ill-health. Yet they also offer hope, because they show that human instinct is alive and well, and telling us that there is something wrong. The violent, anti-social human resembles the caged bird that plucks its feathers or attacks its owner, because it is not allowed to express its true nature in captivity – it has lost touch with its Kannagara.

The search for Kannagara is as instinctive, and beyond words, as the revolt against spiritual and emotional captivity. So much so that it is useful to think of anti-social behavior and the epidemic of anxiety and depression as the dark side of the spiritual quest, arising from the same source. But in the context of Shinto, 'instinct' is not quite the right word, because we need to go beyond biology and psychology. These are manifestations of Kannagara, or rather our relationship to it. They are not Kannagara itself. Kannagara is primal awareness of what is benign within nature therefore ethically 'right'. It is being true to the spirit of nature and therefore the human spirit.

The problem with the growth-based economy and society is that the growth is inorganic and so out of tune with Great Nature. In Shinto, Great Nature has all of the qualities of Kami. At the same time, all manifestations of Kami arise from Great Nature and are part of it. As an organic religion, shaped by ethnic and cultural identity, geography and landscape, Shinto feels and understands the connection between the divine spirit and the natural world. For obvious reasons, ethnic or native faith traditions avoid abstract generalization. They are rooted in the specific. However they express universal truths in ways that reflect the conditions in which they have evolved. Those Arctic peoples who worship their prey do not see life as 'beginning' in one place and 'ending' somewhere else. Life is a continuous thread that links all living systems together. As energy, it can neither be created nor destroyed but passes from one form to another.

And so Arctic peoples have an intuitive understanding of the food chain, to which they give a spiritual meaning, because they draw no clear boundaries between the spiritual and the material realms, seeing them as intertwined. In the same way, traditional African faiths often use for religious purposes objects such as carved stools that serve everyday functions as well. There is no reason why everyday life should be separated from the sacred realm, of which it is part. This understanding is what Shinto calls awareness of Kannagara-no-Michi: the Way in accordance with Kami within Great Nature.

The indigenous world view does not separate the sacred from the mundane. At the same time, it allows insights into upper and lower worlds, or parallel universes that are not so easily understood by societies reliant on abstract reason. The strength of shamanic cultures is that they are able to find hidden connections between natural phenomena. Such abilities are latent in the human race, but are only now being rediscovered by rational science. This is leading to a questioning of western values within the west itself.

Kannagara, then, is Shinto's expression of the indigenous world view. The divine presence is experienced in the landscape of Japan – in snow-capped mountains, rivers and freezing-cold waterfalls, in the seas that surround the archipelago. Water is integral to every Shinto ritual, reflecting the ecology and climate of Japan, the process of inner and outer cleansing. Yet the centrality of water also signifies its centrality to all of life. The Earth, like our bodies, consists largely of water, which connects all living systems because they contain and depend on it. Kannagara is like the flow of water that blurs all divisions and transcends all boundaries. Spiritual practice within Shinto involves 'becoming like water' and so acting in accordance with our true nature without putting up artificial barriers. We are back to the image of 'going with the flow'.

The indigenous spiritual pathways all emphasize connectedness. Water is a powerful image. Each 'drop' of water is part of the flow of the river or the ocean: it is connected to all water everywhere. Another image is the web of life. Central to Germanic spirituality is the concept of *Wyrd*. This means not only fate or destiny for the individual, or society, but also the strands that connect together everything in the universe: the 'Web of Wyrd'.[62] The word Wyrd is related, in Old English, to the word *worethan*, to become, implying the constant state of flux and subtle change within the evolutionary cycle. Karma, in the Indic traditions, is also frequently pictured as a cosmic web. As the universal law of cause and effect, the meaning of karma is that every action impacts on every other action and so there is no such thing as separation.

Kannagara is also about the absence of boundaries between man and nature, and between human beings themselves. It is an inner compass that takes us back to our- selves through realignment with Great Nature. For the loss of that connection is the cause of human unhappiness and lack of spiritual growth: bad karma. Spiritual awakening is a process of opening our hearts to Kannagara so that we are able to find our way back to nature. And far from descent into 'primitivism', realignment with nature is the way to realize our potential, both as individual human beings and as a human civilization.

The Search for the Hidden Mind

In Chinese Daoist teachings, the Dao is sometimes referred to as a Hidden Mind. The Dao, 'formless but complete', is the undifferentiated wholeness that existed before the universe as we know it came into being. However it still exists within all of life and to 'know' it is a return to the point of origin. Dao is both the Way towards enlightenment and the principle of enlightenment itself. It is identified with quiet, subtlety and restraint. Real intelligence is not measured by academic prowess or formal education, but by the ability to live within the benign limits set by nature. Truth is realized by intellectual restraint as well, by realizing that no one has a monopoly of truth that permits them to coerce others, mentally or physically. As Lao Tse reminds us: 'He who knows does not speak, he who speaks does not know'. Therefore the starting point, the journey itself and the arrival all represent aspects of the Dao. It is about the reconciliation of opposites, the recognition of unity in diversity.

The idea of Dao (or Tao, to give the word its more familiar rendering) has come to exert a powerful hold on the imagination of the west, almost more than in East Asia where they originate. The Yin and Yang sign has acquired iconic status and is a familiar symbol of peace, reconciliation and balance. It represents the reconciliation of the two polarities that arose from original Dao. The principle of energy and creativity – the Yang energy – is represented by the white wave, whereas its black counterpart signifies Yin, the passive, subtle, nurturing power. Yin and Yang are also variously identified with soft and hard, feminine and masculine, Heaven and Earth, dark and light, continuity and change. Crucially, each contains an element of the other, represented by the circles of white surrounded by black and black surrounded by white. Each energy source, each apparently polarized principle, contains within it an element of the other and so is not really 'opposite' at all. It is significant that the Yin and Yang principles are depicted in the form of waves that merge

and overlap with each other, rather than as rigid, clearly demar-
cated lines. Just by looking at the Yin-Yang symbol, we gain
insights into a way of thinking different from the adversarial
thought processes to which we in the west have become too
accustomed.

In this way, the Dao provides a point of entry into another way
of looking at the universe. It is an approach that need not be
classified as exclusively 'eastern', because it was once our
approach in the west and could be once again. Dao itself is in
many respects a literate and philosophical rendering of the
ancient shamanic awareness of upper, middle and lower worlds
and the need to reintegrate them to achieve wholeness. And so it
is relevant at three levels to an understanding of Shinto
consciousness. First, an understanding of the Yin-Yang polarity –
and reconciliation – helps us to understand the Shinto approach
to life, which is about shades of meaning instead of straight lines
of thought, *growing together* rather than *standing apart*. Secondly,
Daoism has influenced Japanese and Shinto thinking over many
centuries, along with many other aspects of Chinese thought,
notably Confucianism and Buddhism, which found fertile soil.
Shinto instinctively includes new ideas, rather than putting up
mental drawbridges. That an idea comes from Daoism (or, for
that matter, Hinduism or Christianity) does not mean that it
cannot be, or become, part of Shinto as well. This is viewed as
part of spiritual evolution, which is as natural a process as
physical evolution.

Third, the idea of the Dao is already a powerful force within
Shinto consciousness. Shinto *is* a Dao. As we have already seen,
the 'To' of Shinto is the same as the word Dao, signifying Way or
path. It was Chinese influence that gave rise to 'Shinto' as a verbal
expression, both to distinguish the older faith from the Buddhist
dharma and as an expression of Daoist influence. The emergence
of Shin To, the Way of Kami, marked the transition from a series
of beliefs, local traditions and variegated deities to a literate,

unified faith with its own corpus and its own hierarchies. It is the marriage (*Musubi*) of intuition and scholarship, rural folk custom and urban 'civilization'.

In Shinto, the idea of Dao is expressed in its own way by Kannagara-no-Michi, the Way of attuning oneself to Kami. Kannagara absorbs both yin and yang influences.

Often, it is expressed by Shinto priests and scholars through the union of polarities

Grand Master Yamamoto speaks of the 'vertical musubi' (sic) of Kannagara, which is rooted in popular consciousness of the divine spirit. This contrasts with the 'horizontal musubi', the 'facts' and principles transmitted from above by the Guji, Kannushi and religious scholars. These form a system of belief and practice, but the core of that system is *kokoro*, the heart. Musubi in this context means organic spiritual growth. The union (Musubi as marriage!) between vertical and horizontal principles is likened in turn to warp and woof in the design of a building.

Vertical musubi is identified with Kannagara, as attunement to the divine in nature and the self. Kannagara is the search for the divine in three ways:

- The wish to rise to the level of the divine
- The wish to bring the divine 'down to earth' – in other words, to human and natural levels
- The wish to achieve a sense of identity or union with the divine

According, to Yamamoto, Kannagara is therefore 'the attempt to bring the kami, the divine into direct relation with humans'.[63] It is the union, or more accurately the dissolution of boundaries, between the spiritual world (yin) and the temporal world (yang). He cites the example of the Sakaki tree, an evergreen native to Japan and found nowhere else that is held to be sacred. Kami 'alights' on the Sakaki 'so that people may commune with' the divine spirit. The Sakaki is a natural instrument through which people tune in to Kami, so that either a specific deity or the underlying principle of divine energy 'can be invited to alight there', or 'on any purified place'.[64]

The Sakaki tree becomes a point of entry for Kami to human consciousness. Kami power is brought down to earth by humans when they focus on it, using the tree. At the same time, humans use the tree to rise to the level of Kami, to realize the Kami power within themselves. It is mundane, part of the everyday natural world, but it is also sacred because it contains the 'invited' Kami, enabling us to communicate with forces that shape our lives and yet are usually hidden and invisible. The Sakaki is the expression of Dai Shizen, the greatness of nature by which we come to recognize the sacred dimensions ordinary life. And Dai Shizen is a form of Kami energy in itself.

It is noticeable that the Yin-Yang polarities are united by this process, but at the same time remain distinct. This might seem puzzling to the secular-rationalist mindset, but it is the spirit of Kannagara, defying conventional logic. Thus the Sakaki is simultaneously distinct from and at one with Kami. Nature itself is simultaneously divine and mundane and humans are both mortal men and women and Kami, anchored equally in 'earthly' and 'heavenly' realms. Both realms continuously interact and *flow into* each other. Kannagara is the process through which we see this happen, by which new dimensions and new possibilities are opened to us.

In this spirit of interaction, the horizontal musubi is as much a part of Kannagara as the vertical, although the role of the latter is emphasized by Yamamoto. The warp and woof are equally crucial to construction, and in the same way neither musubi is more important than the other. Kannagara consists of two dimensions or forces. These can be expressed in the following terms:

- Vertical and Horizontal
- Light and Darkness
- Up and Down
- Right and Left

'It is the blend [of these, and innumerable other natural polarities] that creates Kannagara.'[65] Through this blending, each element retains its own properties but at the same time contributes to something larger than itself. By the same principle, the Shinto practitioner does not dismiss the teachings of any other religion simply because the conclusions might be different from his. Such dismissal would be run against the entire spirit of Shinto and signify detachment from Kannagara. This principle applies outside the sphere of religion to imply respect for all expressions of human culture. Men and women of Michi need not refrain from just and courteous criticisms of other cultures, and their own. But they will recognize that all cultures, like all spiritual paths, spring from the same source and are intertwined. To force one culture or belief system on another therefore disrupts nature's warp and woof – and so causes suffering to the oppressed and oppressors alike.

Equally, Kami are simultaneously Many and One. Recognition of one 'individual' Kami is therefore also recognition of all Kami and vice versa, and Kami is both plural and singular – the undifferentiated force behind the universe and its myriad parts. Kami are at the same time their human, animal, plant or mineral forms *and* the invisible energies beneath them. Each expression of Kami flows into each other expression of Kami. Past flows into present and into future, which is why Shinto is known as the religion of the 'middle-now', 'eternal present' or 'here and now': the *naka-ima*. This means that consciousness of the present incorporates and absorbs the past and the future, without which the present is meaningless or non-existent. The principle of becoming like water guides the relationship between the cycles of time and evolution, humans and Kami, Kami and nature, Kami and itself.

Most of the Kannushi interviewed by Jean Herbert associate Kannagara with the abolition of any division between 'what we call material and what we call spiritual'.[66] It can be seen as the equivalent of yoga, in the Hindu tradition, meaning union – the joining of the human spirit with the divine power. Except, of course, that in Shinto neither aspect cancels the other out. The spiritual does not invalidate the material and nor does the divine cancel out the human. Instead, they exert a modifying, tempering influence on each other.

Kami is thereby humanized, whereas humanity is transported to its highest level and fulfils its true potential. According to Harada, through Kannagara-no-Michi, 'human life [is] linked with the superhuman'.[67] This can mean the link between human and Kami, but more indirectly it means that Shinto does not draw the same distinction as western cultures between the 'natural' and the 'supernatural'. Observable material beings and the spirit world are continuous rather than separate. Shinto, like ancient Greek or Northern European paganism, has an infinite variety of nature spirits, ghosts, fairy beings and wights, linked mostly to ecosystems and natural phenomena. These are just as 'real' – and just as infused with Kami energy – as the material beings they influence and are influenced by in turn. Kannagara equips us with the perception of these shadow worlds. Once again, it mirrors modern science, which uncovers layers of reality we did not know were present. This aspect of science is a manifestation of Kannagara, which is why true reason is 'the essence of Michi'. Reason only assumes its true form when it unites with intuitive understanding. These two polarities are also the warp and woof of human consciousness.

Different levels of understanding are expressed in different ways, by different philosophies. We have seen that 'being Shinto' encompasses acceptance of other spiritual paths. Within Japanese religious culture, Confucianism has been interpreted as the Michi (Way) of scholars and sages, Buddhism as the Michi of Buddha and Shinto itself as the Michi of Kami. They remain three distinct strands of thought, and they repeatedly interact and overlap. It has been frequently observed that many Japanese favor Shinto weddings and Buddhist funerals. Shinto is associated with life and its affirmation in the present ('the middle now'), Buddhism with the cycles of death and rebirth: the karmic process. The practice of Buddhism (or any other religion) in certain contexts in no way implies estrangement from Shinto. Confucianism, meanwhile, is linked to the legal and political structures that give solid form to the original impulse behind human fellowship: Kannagara-no-Michi.

A Moral Aesthetic

Kannagara unites the human with the divine realms, exposing the divisions between them as a temporary illusion, a barrier put up by humans who do not know themselves. This alignment is achieved through the realignment of humanity with nature. The division between humankind and the natural world, and the illusion of superiority and 'dominion' over nature, is as dangerous a form of false consciousness as the illusion of inferiority to Kami. The spiritually-attuned man or woman recognizes the Kami energy equally within the self and within the Great Nature of which that self is part. This is essential to the union – Musubi – of the material and spiritual worlds, and in Shinto that is the purpose of all spiritual practice, the height of spiritual evolution. Kannagara (under whatever name) is the oldest human impulse, but it is also the most advanced human idea, the beginning and end of the cycle of life.

Therefore the Way (Michi), by which an ethical life is achieved, is found by tuning into nature and recognizing its inherent moral wealth. Central to Shinto is the idea that nature, including human nature, is inherently good. In this it differs

105

from most religious traditions, including mainstream Buddhism, Hinduism and Christianity. There, salvation is achieved by turning away from or transcending natural impulses, which are associated with baseness, materialism or lack of awareness. Shinto comes at the question of human nature (and humanity within nature) from the opposite perspective. Humans are indeed 'born free' in the sense that their natural inclinations are good, pure and therefore moral. There is no 'original sin', no primal corruption arising from the natural world. Moral error, identified with impurity, arises from estrangement from nature or resistance to its flow. The morality of Kannagara is 'an unconscious observance of the Way':[68]

> To act in accord with the course of nature, without conscious effort, obedient to the impulse of constitutional prompting, is the highest virtue in Shinto eyes.[69]

The moral sensibility of Shinto arises through a process of surrendering to nature. This means the 'external' world of animals, rivers, seas and mountains. The spirit of that external nature is expressed in our response of quiet reverence to the life-affirming properties of 'flowers, pure snow, soft rains, gentle breeze'. These, like all natural forms, become access points to Kami. When we react to the 'silent and provocative beauty of the natural order', we become aware of Kannagara.[70]

Equally, the nature to which we surrender is our own true nature, our inner landscape, to which we give way. Kannagara is viewed as a primal, unwritten law which is on a higher plane than man-made legal codes, necessary though those might be. Yet, again paradoxically, it is our very ability to comprehend our inner nature and live accordingly that gives human beings their special talents. Motoori Norinaga even argues that the appreciation of Kannagara differentiates us from animals that 'require rules'.[71] This is how Kannagara is different from pure 'instinct'.

Rather than simply reacting to the world around them, humans in touch with their true nature achieve an inner understanding that can be expressed both emotionally and intellectually. Such response to nature is expressed through painting, music, philosophy and literature: the creativity of Musubi. It is found in worship, meditation and the spiritual sensibility that arises from walking in a forest or climbing a mountain and looking downwards.

By tuning ourselves to Kannagara, we unlock the Kami power inside us and it is realized through human creativity. That includes technological innovation, and all that makes life enjoyable and interesting, as long as it is not wasteful or excessive. In Shinto, there is no polarization of nature and technology. Kannagara brings them together, just as it brings together the spiritual and the material. The test is whether technological progress is used for peaceful means and to improve the quality of life. Where this is the case, it is part of the flow of nature. Where it is used as an instrument of destruction, a weapon against fellow humans or Great Nature itself, it is contrary to Kannagara and so in defiance of the inner moral law. And any attack on Great Nature always has destructive consequences for humankind.

Shinto thereby brings the nature-centered philosophy of an ancient indigenous culture into the context of one of the most highly technological and urbanized civilizations in the world. Its continuity shows us that the values associated with indigenous societies – largely isolated and using traditional technologies – are relevant to our own society and to the planet. By adopting them, we go forward rather than 'going back'. We learn to live restrained and sustainable, but fulfilled and enjoyable lives. Kannagara also reminds us that co-operation between human beings is, in reality, the highest evolutionary principle, because it guarantees our survival and advancement as human beings.

That is the morality of nature. We have noted that the

principle of Kannagara unites the moral and aesthetic sensibil-
ities: awareness of our inner nature with response to nature's
outer beauty. From the standpoint we are used to in the west, this
might seem to be evidence of naivety. Nature, after all, can be
frightening, destructive and terrible in the literal sense. Shinto
consciousness is aware of the frightening aspects of nature,
which are as much manifestations of Kami as the obviously
benign. As humans, we use our intelligence and creativity to
protect ourselves from these aspects of nature's power. But in
contrast to the (failing but still dominant) western approach of
merely erecting barriers, the Shinto approach to protecting
ourselves from arbitrary natural forces is looking at nature with
a sense of respect and awe. We therefore learn to co-operate with
those natural forces that might overwhelm us by co-operating
with them and knowing our limitations. Shinto consciousness
also understands that our own arbitrary behavior, our despoliation of the environment, comes back on us and threatens our
well-being, even our survival as a species. Kannagara is the most
ancient form of ecological consciousness, but at no time has it
been as relevant as in our technological age.

The logic at the heart of Kannagara is ultimately quite
straightforward. It arises out of an original human awareness of
interconnectedness. Trees sustain life, for example, and as such
become sacred repositories of Kami energy. We are part of a web
that connects all living things, and also binds together past,
present and future in the 'middle now'. Each succeeding generation and each evolutionary phase arises from what has gone
before and gives way to something that is new and distinct, but
contains all previous influences. Human intelligence is realized
through awareness of these processes, whether that is through
genetics and neuroscience or spiritual practice. Both should lead
to the same place, which is knowledge of the Kami power within
us. Humans are children of the sun and so have an inner light
that enables them to grow physically, mentally and as spiritual

beings. That growth should be organic and in accordance with Great Nature's cycles of continuity and change. It is here that the concept of Musubi emerges to guide humanity.

Chapter Five: Musubi –
Spiritual Ecology

*Since Shinto is the way of the Kami, or the stream of life from the gods, its myths should be understood as they stand or "live" without any ideological resolution. They should be construed through the logic of **musubi**, i.e. the growing, nourishing and creative life.*
Hirata Atsutane

Being and Becoming: The Meanings of Musubi

Musubi is the most enlightening word in Shinto.
J.W.T. Mason[72]

Musubi is the first principle that gives life to everything in the universe. It is the energy that gives form and character to all that is alive and that ensures continuity from one living being, one species and one evolutionary form to another. It is the shared experience that connects ancestors and descendants for all of time. Musubi is the organic process of development and growth. We witness it in the flower that turns towards the light and opens, in the cry of the newborn child, in the spread of moss over damp stones. But we see it equally in the processes of ageing and dying, in the autumn and winter as much as in spring and summer. For Musubi is the natural cycle of life, decline and renewal, connecting each individual life to its predecessors and successors. Musubi is expressed equally through individual creativity and group co-operation, individual life and the collective lives of peoples or species.

Musubi is the life force contained in nature. Some would say that it *is* nature, because everything within nature is Musubi. However it is also at the heart of a spiritual understanding of the

Earth and the universe, encompassing Kami and nature spirits as much as flora and fauna. In this sense, the concept of Musubi broadens our definition, and understanding, of nature and life energy. It extends the idea of life to things that are not immediately visible or explicable. Therefore Musubi, like Kannagara, is as much a scientific as a spiritual concept. The invention of the microscope, for instance, has made humanity aware of many layers of life that are not visible to the naked eye, but (as in the case of viruses) can exert enormous and terrifying power over us. The science of astronomy has given us a new understanding of the planets and stars, and their impact on us – and opened up many new mysteries along the way. Through the science of ecology, we have come to appreciate the importance of micro-organisms and deep-sea creatures and the hidden connections between living systems. We have come to understand the importance of maintaining nature's balance, and that when we disrupt that balance we can disrupt the climate and the sources of food and water: in other words, all that sustains life. Such understanding is an appreciation of Musubi.

The importance of Musubi to the Shinto practitioner is that it brings different levels of consciousness together, just as rational science connects different levels of reality. Through Musubi, life energy is therefore connected with Kami energy, whether that is identified with individual, anthropomorphized deities or the creative power of the universe. Musubi connects divine energy – Kami consciousness – to trees, rocks, streams and mountains. It makes humans conscious of nature spirits and elemental beings, such as *djinn* in Islamic cultures, faeries in the Celtic tradition or the *Leshy* in Slavic paganism, whether they are literally 'believed in' or not. In Japan, there are countless nature spirits and the spiritual powers of animals – members of the dog family a notable example – are acknowledged as much today as they were millennia ago.

W.G. Aston, an Englishman writing just after the height of

western colonial arrogance, used this ability to move between levels of consciousness as evidence that the Japanese were more 'neglectful' than the west of the 'distinction between the animate and the inanimate'.[73] His words were informed by a mixture of Judeo-Christian prejudice and mechanistic, linear thinking, both of which were already beginning to be questioned at the start of the twentieth century. In fact, it showed a deeper appreciation of reality than that which still remains dominant in western thinking.

In 1967, the radical psychiatrist R.D. Laing asked in his essay 'The Politics of Experience': 'who could be so superstitious as to suppose that the soul does not exist because we cannot see it at the end of a microscope?'[74] He was identifying the problem that arises when science is turned into a superstition. Then, a fundamentalist approach to reason fails to accept anything beyond the material and the quantifiable. This makes science and reason self-limiting and so destroys their original purpose, which is to broaden human understanding and increase human potential. The Shinto worldview offers a healthy corrective to this approach, because its aim is to bring the spiritual and the material dimensions of life into harmony and, as part of this process, make them communicate with each other.

Moreover, the purpose of the 'anti-psychiatry' movement of which Laing was part was to question prevailing western notions of sanity, which were rooted in mechanistic assumptions about human society and the nature of reality. In Shinto, it is taken as a given that reality has many facets and levels, some of which might appear contradictory or confusing. That, for the Shinto practitioner, is the nature of life and is part of the workings of Musubi. Through Musubi, the different levels of reality are brought together and reconciled.

Therefore Musubi is at once a natural principle of organic growth and a connecting principle by which the worlds of humanity and Kami are brought together. This process of 'bringing together' is fundamental to Musubi, at every level where the concept is applied. And Musubi is also the process by which life continues as a series of 'endless conversions and evolutions', so that there is no ultimate 'death', merely a transfer of life from one form to another. In 1958, the *Jinja Honcho* (Shrine Association of Japan) defined Musubi as 'the spirit of birth and becoming; also birth, accomplishment; the creating and harmonizing powers'.[75]

Musubi is the key to Shinto, and yet it has many meanings and implications, which continuously overlap and interact with each other. Often, they might appear contradictory to the western mindset. Yet the key to understanding Musubi is to let go of the critical faculties that we sometimes overvalue. We are asked, in effect, to allow the process of organic growth to take over and to be guided by it, rather than trying to impose on it our own preconceptions or blueprints. Musubi is the principle behind all of Shinto thought and practice, usually remaining in the background or the unconscious, but giving shape and definition to everything else within the Shinto tradition.

From the standpoint of Shinto, the unconscious is the place where the worlds of spirit and matter, dreaming and waking are brought together. It is a *collective* unconscious, in that it is a repository of genetic and cultural memories, but at the same time it is an *individual* unconscious, shaped by personal experiences, characteristics and desires. Thus the unconscious in Shinto encompasses the both the Jungian and Freudian interpretations, but is also something much more: the receptacle for spiritual insight and the point of access to Kami power. It is not to be feared or suppressed, but nurtured and cultivated. The unconscious is part of the self, but at the same time connects us to forces much larger than the self: the natural world, the spiritual universe and our fellow human beings. By letting the unconscious take over, we understand the workings of Musubi as a natural process and a spiritual path. And so, when we are 'neglectful' of the 'distinction between the animate and the inanimate', we erase artificial barriers and gain clearer insights into the ways in which aspects of the universe connect with each other. This is Musubi as a form of spiritual science. Far from expressing a more 'primitive' consciousness, it offers us a vision of the universe – and human society – more 'advanced' than the failed mechanistic models we are now trying to leave behind.

In attempt to convey the idea of Musubi to the west, Jean Herbert focuses on a popular Shinto symbol, the 'three comma-shaped figures in a whirl' as the 'triad of dynamic movements of musubi [sic]'[76]: expansion, contraction, completion or synthesis. Through Musubi, we understand nature as a series of continuous cycles rather than discrete phases. We visualize the principle of life as a spiral, like the DNA helix, rather than a series of steps or a straight line. And we see evolution in these terms as well, so that all living systems are intimately linked. They are points on the spiral that fulfill distinctive but equally crucial roles. The focus shifts from exploring differences (between species, ecosystems and human groups, for instance) to exploring similarities and common interests. The concept of the spiral also makes us aware of the continuity of life. Each living thing is the sum total of its evolutionary inheritance as well as existing in its own right. Moreover, as well as making its own unique contribution to the pervasive life force – Musubi – that life form will give way to or develop into something else. This takes place at several different levels:

- The process of development, growth and regression that takes place during the life of an individual organism. This can include development at physical, psychic and spiritual, intellectual and experiential levels.
- Reproduction, which provides for continuity (and change) between the generations: it is a thread that connects past, present and future.

- Individual creativity, contribution to the wider community, relationships of love, friendship and fellowship.
- The experience of death, which from the standpoint of Musubi is the reintegration with the source of life, Dai Shizen or Great Nature. It is the end of one cycle, from which a new one emerges.

The list is equally applicable to humans, other animal species, plants and minerals. All of these things are animated by Musubi and united by the principle of life. Kami are animated by Musubi too: indeed they can be said to embody it. Therefore, it is through Musubi that we arrive at an understanding of the divine, which is itself subject to the principle of Musubi. To the Shinto way of thinking, this is no paradox. For Shinto is about unity and alignment rather than separation and difference. From the Shinto perspective, 'is' and 'is not', 'either/or' create confusion rather than clarity.

Evolution itself is a manifestation of Musubi. This can mean the evolution of a species, or the transformation of one species into another over eons (which are trivial in Musubi-time!). It can mean the social development of a community or society. And it can also mean the creative, personal or spiritual evolution of an individual. Musubi is at once the process of evolution and our awareness of that process. Through Musubi consciousness, we understand the unique characteristics of each life form *and* the unity of all life. In turn, we understand that all life is interdependent and find our place within nature's tapestry.

Through Musubi, we see the natural cycle as a balance of continuity and change. Rather than opposing each other (another frequent western assumption), these two principles interact and fluctuate. They need each other to support the life generated by their union. We can identify continuity and change with the Yin and Yang polarities. Each contains a crucial element

115

of the other, each one yields to the other in a perpetual cycle of existence. We observe this process in the phases of the moon, for example, and the changes in the seasons. Subtle shifts can increase our awareness. An impression of warmth during the cold months and a hint of cool, crisp weather during the hot season both denote changes to come. The seed that stays alive through the winter months and waits to break into flower is the element of Yang within the Yin. The clear, cold late summer night is the Yin to which the Yang will soon give way. Continuity is Yin, change is Yang. Both principles need each other to exist in their own right and feed off each other to survive. The cells within each human body develop, die and are replenished roughly every seven years, making each human simultaneously different and the same. This is the operation of Musubi and it is replicated within all living systems.

We can therefore see Musubi as the point at which the Yin and Yang principles come together. Or we can see it as a knot that binds together the vital threads of continuity and change that unite everything in the universe. One of the literal meanings of Musubi is 'knot' and the word also implies the process of binding or *tying* together. This is also the way in which reproduction of all types takes place and so the word Musubi also connotes reproducing or begetting: *musu*, to 'beget' (as in *musuko*, son and *musume*, daughter) and *bi*, an old word denoting all that is wonderful, honorable or miraculous – and the divine sun, from which all these things flow. *Umusu* is the act of begetting. In this context, we need to remember that the Shinto tradition regards all life – and the original principle of life - as inherently worthy of honor and respect. It follows then that Musubi is the process of continuous unification and replication by which all life forms comes into being, grows and matures and is transformed into other living things. Musubi is identified with the sun's light, which allows life to come into being, then sustains and transforms it. Hirata thereby defines it as 'a dynamic power uniting a pair of correlative opposites such as man and woman, day and night, and subject and object'.[77] Musubi is at once the principle and the process of these unifications – and the new forms that stem from them. It is the origin of life and the continuity of life at the same time.

Another, quite similar meaning of Musubi is associated with the words *musu* meaning to brew or ferment, and *bi* (or sometimes *hi*) denoting the sun, fire, light, and the soul, or the divine power that encapsulates all these forces. This illustrates the ability of Shinto to identify the most subtle and complex spiritual powers with basic natural activities or mundane and entirely secular human actions, such as the brewing of *sake*, the Japanese rice wine. For it is through such actions as brewing, or indeed sexual reproduction, that the spiritual and material worlds come together and interlock: yet another definition of *Musubi*! Professor Chiko Fujisawa identifies Musubi with *mi*, or 'three', which has a spiritual meaning denoting the three under-lying powers of expansion, contraction and evolution mentioned above. It is the process by which the sun generates all beings, 'animate and inanimate'[78] and all beings eventually return to the point of origin of life to re-emerge in new forms.

Yet another meaning of Musubi is conclusion or synthesis, the result of the tying together or unification of different forms of life. This is the balancing of polarities that leads to equilibrium within nature or the human person. But from this conclusion, the process of division, unification and replication always begins anew. And Musubi also means marriage, partnership or coupling. This encompasses equally the sexual and erotic aspects of coupling, the act of commitment and the intellectual or spiritual (in western terms 'platonic') association. It includes arousal and reproduction, applies equally to humans and other animal species (and plants, as in the process of pollination), and beyond that the coupling of humankind and Kami, which is the aim of all spiritual practice.[79] Individual and collective worship or meditation in Shinto is about bringing humans and Kami onto the same plane of consciousness: a tying of the knot, a *Musubi*, between human and divine intelligence.

In becoming aware of Musubi, we recognize the subtle shifts – and continuities – between singular and plural, being and becoming, the cycles of nature, the seasons and life/death/rebirth. We understand Musubi through surrendering to it or accepting it more than by a process of abstract reason. We *feel* it much as we feel the sun's warmth or the cool breeze against our faces. Musubi transcends reason, but at the same time provides for a synthesis, another tying of the knot, between rational thought and the intuitive imagination. It is as if, for example, Shinto practitioners knew many centuries before verification by science that the cells in the body are constantly dying off and re-forming themselves, so that each human being remains the same but is continuously transformed. While the essential 'self' continues, the composition of that self is never precisely the same. This interaction (Musubi) of continuity and change continues through the life of every living being and accompanies the processes of growth, physical or spiritual development, ageing and decline, followed immediately by new growth.

All this was indeed 'known' to Shinto, at the level of intuitive understanding. In much the same way, shamanic cultures understand the evolutionary links between humanity and the animal world, expressing them through 'shape-shifting' transformations between man and beast. The Way of Kami is the same tradition as shamanic or indigenous spirituality. It has adapted to a technology-based urban setting because the concept of Musubi has enabled Shinto to grow organically like nature itself and the evolution of human knowledge. And so in the technological era, ancient spiritual intuition is united with scientific understanding. By the tying of this Musubi-knot, spirituality is given scientific foundations and science acquires a spiritual base. That is an example of Kami and human consciousness uniting, so that the creativity of each is fully expressed.

Like the most ancient forms of faith, and the most modern scientific insights, Shinto begins from the assumption that all is connected. Great Nature is 'the context of life beyond the particular circumstances of the moment'.[80] It includes not only humans and animals, but the whole of the natural world, including the lowliest life-forms (to superficial human eyes), which are in reality complex and profoundly significant to the survival of all life. Moreover it extends beyond Planet Earth to include the entire universe. Kami power is as much a part of Great Nature as material life forms. This is why a sense of Musubi brings together the material and spiritual powers and gives us points of contact with Kami. Sacred trees, rocks or mountain springs are portals for cosmic or Kami energy, which is allied to the life force of Musubi.

Natural formations such as these become centers of Kami power because they embody the natural process of organic growth. They stay the same but change and continuously adapt. Water eternally replenishes itself, rocks move and erode but remain solid, the landscape and vegetation of a mountain evolves and adapts with the climate and seasons. The orbit of the Earth changes almost imperceptibly. Tectonic plates move beneath the planet surface, changing landscapes and forging new continents over eons. All these changes and continuities are expressions of Musubi. For humans, Musubi is an understanding that these changes are inevitable, but that beneath them there is the constancy of the life force. The continuity between nature and Shinto shrines is expressed through the construction of shrines from wood, which needs to be frequently patched up or replaced to reflect different phases of the cycle of life. The great Ise Jinja is demolished and rebuilt completely every twenty years to signify the process of renewal: the same structure, made from new parts; the same body, composed of different cells.

Awareness of Musubi means an understanding that everything in the universe is connected. It is awareness of the web of life, as modern ecologists call it, or *Wyrd* as it was understood by the ancient inhabitants of northern Europe. Native Americans have similar concepts, such as *Wakan*, meaning sacred and natural, whilst Mongolian peoples are guided by the idea of *Tegsh*, which means both understanding of nature's balance and a willingness to live in balance with nature.[81] Kannagara, as we have already seen, is the process by which we become attuned to nature's rhythms, which are also the rhythms of Kami. Therefore Kannagara and Musubi overlap. They are not separate from each other, but different expressions of the same consciousness, or different angles of perception. Grand Master Yamamoto describes Kannagara as a type of Musubi, but equally a sense of Musubi can be seen as an expression of Kannagara consciousness. For Yamamoto, a 'vertical musubi' (sic) involves 'the transmission of life from the past to the present'[82] and for most Shinto practitioners this process extends indefinitely into the future.

Equally, we are reminded that the individual is not an isolated, autonomous unit (as is too often assumed today), but connected to all other humans and, by extension, to all of life, by the workings of nature and by a sacred Musubi-knot. Through that union with the rest of life, we gain the creative potential that leads to individual fulfillment. But by isolating ourselves, as a species, as a racial group or merely as individuals, we lose that creativity or transform it into a destructive power.

Musubi should be seen as an unbroken chain that unites those who live today with those who lived before and those who have yet to be born. And it also pulls towards the center all the connected strands within the web of life. As spiritually conscious humans, we become aware of our need to tread carefully, to live as simply as possible in a way that is attuned to nature's ways. This is because our actions are part of the continuing spiral of creation. Each act, however seemingly trivial, connects with (and can improve on or undermine) each of our previous actions. More than that, every decision we make impacts directly on our contemporaries and our successors alike, all of whom are united with us in Great Nature.

We have spoken of Grand Master Yamamoto's likening of the 'vertical' and 'horizontal' Musubi powers to the warp and woof in the construction of a building. The warp is 'constant and continuing', a thread that must be 'long, steady, regular and firm'. The woof, meanwhile, 'makes the actual design reflecting the time, era and circumstances'. With the warp as a solid basis, the woof 'can act with freedom'. Horizontal musubi (sic) is 'transmitted from above' by scholars and priests, but it evolves and adapts to its surroundings and becomes part of a changing, evolving folk culture of myth, legend, ritual, with traditions that act as centers of stability. Vertical musubi is the spiritual background, the consistently enduring Kami power and 'the attempt to bring the kami (sic), the divine into direct relation with humans'. The core of vertical musubi is *kokoro*, the heart, the center of spiritual awareness as well as the generator of life within the body – and the flow of blood, which is also the flow of Kannagara.

Vertical musubi, the expression of underlying Kami power, gives way to cultural creativity, from which can arise an understanding of the universe and the divine spirit in nature. Such creativity can be expressed through language, art and music, or by science, by collective worship or by private acts of meditation and the inspiration that comes from feeling 'at one' with nature. Tradition gives creativity its basis of stability: 'Once created, [spiritual] traditions can be transmitted through the horizontal *musubi*'. They can adapt and be transformed, in the same way as the best abstract painters have benefited from a classical training.

In this way, the warp and the woof, the vertical and horizontal principles of Musubi are as 'correct, useful [and] valid' as each other. There is no sense in trying to compare or contrast their uses or suggest that one is more important, for the two are mutually dependent and intertwined. Kannagara indeed unites these two 'forces': it brings together vertical and horizontal, light and darkness, up and down, right and left'. Through Musubi, the principle and act of union, opposites are reconciled and 'it is the blend that creates *kannagara* [sic]'.

'Vertical' and 'horizontal' Musubi correspond to the principles of continuity and change that define all of existence. The process of Musubi is one of alignment between different principles within Great Nature and ultimately alignment of material and spiritual powers: the union of the material world with Kami. Musubi is also a process of transformation, whether physical or spiritual. *Musu* is, as we have seen above, identified with the character representing 'steam' or 'brew' and thus the fermentation of sake. As Grand Master Yamakage points out, in the making of sake 'rice or wheat is transformed into something entirely different' and this serves as a metaphor for all other processes of transformation.[83] Sake is frequently drunk at Shinto ceremonies. This is part of the affirmation and celebration of life. At the same time, it is a celebration of Musubi, both as a spiritual principle and a process within nature that is continuously at work.

Yamakage also cites the phrase *koke musu* (literally 'moss grows'), 'which describes the way in which the moss plant emerges suddenly on the surface of a rock'.[84] The principles of creation and transformation, so essential to every aspect of Shinto, can be applied to the inner transformation of the individual, 'the process of work through which each person generates, grows, transforms and develops *naohinomitama* ['nao-hin-omi-tama'] (the innermost pure spirit), making his or her spirit become strong'.[85] Through spiritual cultivation, human beings 'may keep growing until they eventually become Kami'.[86]

That is the esoteric meaning of Musubi: an inner discipline through which humans transform themselves from purely materialistic creatures to spiritually conscious beings. This can take place at the individual level, but it can also apply to whole communities, peoples, nations and the global community. At whichever level, practice involves learning from and following the example of nature, instead of assuming a position of superiority and 'dominion' over it. In the Shinto idea of Musubi, we have the basis of a new global ethic of balance. We also have a spiritual practice that can transform the way modern humanity sees itself and its relationship to the rest of nature – within the world and beyond it. The idea of human beings 'becoming Kami' can mean the realization of full human potential (the divine spark or Kami energy within). Paradoxically, that takes place through an understanding of our one-ness, our continuity with all other natural forms and ecosystems, rather than trying to separate ourselves from them. Transformation also occurs when we realize that all human interests are intimately linked. There is no 'I' without 'We', no singular without the plural. Conversely, there can be no co-operation between human beings without respect for the uniqueness and dignity of each individual, each cell within the collective human body.

The image of moss growing on a rock is one of the most powerful evocations of Musubi within Shinto thought. The moss plant, as Grand Master Yamakage tells us, does 'suddenly emerge' on the rock, yet at all other times it stays alive but dormant, below the surface of ordinary consciousness. As such, it represents the cycle of birth, death and rebirth – a cycle of Musubi – in which all life is caught up. An apparently elementary life form illustrates how all living organisms come into existence and transform themselves, reminding us of our own place in nature. All nature-based faiths recognize this basic cycle of living, and Shinto is able to reconnect its urban, sophisticated followers with natural rhythms that they might otherwise forget. It shows urban men and women that the advantages of technology and science cannot ultimately shield them from nature, and nor should we use them to do so. The true purpose of such knowledge *is* to improve and prolong our lives, but it is also to help us live in a more balanced way and in greater harmony with our surroundings. And so technologies that would seem to point us away from the natural world in fact take us back to Great Nature – and that is, in itself, a process of transformation and synthesis.

From the image of *koke musu* ('moss grows'), we also understand that there is no death, as such, merely a process by which natural forms subside and re-emerge in new form. Nature is constantly renewing and re-inventing itself, even when it appears to remain the same. Transformations occur throughout the lifetime of an organism (as we know well with our own human bodies) and so the transformations that take place after death can be seen as a continuation of this process instead of something wholly new. This is why Shinto sees death as the beginning of something new as well as the end of something old. Death is therefore an integral part of Musubi, the point of contraction whereby a living being declines and fades away and the life energy flows elsewhere.

Yet the transformations that arise from that life energy are many and various. Continuity and change are experienced in the flow of life from one generation to another, both in what we call genetic inheritance and in the personal memories by which our forebears (or departed friends and lovers) 'live on' within us. Ancestors are a genetic and spiritual link with the past, and a reminder of our obligations towards the future. We witness the Musubi of regeneration in the return of the moss to the rock face, in spring flowers and autumn leaves, in the seasonal changes that are each marked within Shinto practice. But there are other, less direct transfers of life energy that are equally sacred. Here we can keep in mind the image of a memorial tree that grows above a human grave. The tree represents the continuation of the life force and its transfer from the human sphere of influence to another realm of nature – a realm, as it happens, that is far more ancient and far more essential to the maintenance of life as a whole.

We have noted that Shinto is vague about death and afterlife. This contrasts it with the monotheistic religions, Christianity and Islam in particular, and with the Indic faiths, such as Buddhism and Hinduism. All these have intricate and highly -evolved concepts of afterlife, whether these take the form of heavenly or hellish domains, or reincarnation until the cycle of birth, death and rebirth (*samsara* in Buddhism) is broken by enlightenment. Secular humanism, as it has developed in the west over recent decades, tends towards the doctrinaire certainty that each individual life is separate, compartmentalized and extinguished completely by physical death. Shinto, by contrast, lacks any such certainties. Unlike the more other-worldly faiths, it is more concerned with the processes of life than the rituals associated with death or too much speculation about 'what comes next'. This has sometimes led to the entirely unfair criticism that Shinto is materialistic in character. The apparent lack of interest in death has also led critics to claim that Shinto is primitive in nature and spiritually underdeveloped. In reality, nothing could be further from the truth. Shinto practitioners are not primarily interested in death because they are aware that Musubi transcends the death of individual organisms. They know that the thread of life persists and that it connects all beings: present, past and future. The 'vagueness' about death is merely an understanding that life is constantly being recycled, often in unexpected ways.

This brings us to the final definition of Musubi: the life force itself. In this context, it is 'nothing other than pure duration, having neither beginning nor end'.[87] Like energy, it can neither be created nor destroyed, but it assumes many forms and can pass freely from one form to another. We have already seen that the Shinto emblem represents, as well as three principles of life, the whirling motion of a continually revolving circle. In this whirl of light, colors merge with each other, lines and boundaries disappear and there is only a continual movement without a beginning, middle or end, a continual flux but also a unity achieved in perpetual motion. In this context, that is the essence of Musubi. It is the animating principle that gives life to all things, the origin and conductor of life that pervades the universe. Musubi is an expression of Kami (and is represented as several Kami deities), but it also gives life to all the expressions of Kami power that guide the universe.[88]

Musubi connects the various planes of consciousness that make up human thought: philosophical and practical; abstract and concrete; material and spiritual; changing and constant. It brings together the intuitive and rational powers, the right and left hemispheres of the brain, the world of dream and the world of scientific deduction. As such it is Shinto's own life force, enabling the timeless faith of an ancient people to adapt and become more relevant than ever to a dynamic, interconnected and increasingly confused planet.

Musubi and Karma

One of Shinto's earliest western admirers, James W.T. Mason, concluded that the concept of Musubi 'eliminates from Shinto a mechanistic philosophy of life under the control of an aloof Deity or dominated by fate or any principle of the inevitability of cause and effect'.[89]

As an American, Mason identified strongly with Shinto's emphasis on individual liberty and freedom of conscience. He approved of the absence of a binding creed, the possibility of experiment and the duty of each individual to work out his or her own moral destiny. This meant attuning him or herself to nature, finding Kannagara, but doing so as a personal spiritual quest, rather than conforming to a fixed doctrine. In other words, it meant spiritual Musubi: organic growth occurring spontaneously and naturally within the individual conscience.

However Mason also admired that aspect of Shinto which contrasted most with American individualism. This was the group ethic, the sense of interdependence between 'I' and 'We', the idea that consensus was vital to human progress. The sense of the collective is equally an expression of Musubi. Human societies, like all natural formations, grow organically. Musubi is as much about consensus between man and nature as consensus between human beings: the latter is an extension of the former. Mason and his contemporaries do not refer much, if at all, to the ecological dimensions of Musubi, because they were not in tune with contemporary western preoccupations: Mason was writing in the 1930s. But they were fascinated by the organic view of society that arose from Shinto consciousness and practice, recalling earlier currents in European thought.

Mason is therefore interesting to us today, because although more scholarly and restrained, his reactions prefigure those of many thoughtful western men and women who have turned towards eastern spiritual pathways. Often, they embrace the 'otherness' of Asian philosophies, but at the same time project onto them exaggerated aspects of western individualistic thinking. There is a temptation to make the now familiar confusion between liberation and libertarianism. This is a cause of considerable cultural misunderstanding. It leads inevitably to disappointment and frustration for many a western seeker, who is unable to break the attachment to narrow definitions of self and self-fulfillment that are the original cause of spiritual and psychic anxiety.

Shinto, like other holistic world views, requires an under-standing of the self in a much wider context, the web of life that connects all beings. This means the ability to grasp that freedom arises from discipline and restraint, which are not the same as authoritarian repression, but its opposite, liberation from within. The purpose of spiritual practice is the alignment of the self with all living systems. True spiritual awareness in Shinto is the

127

conscious and intuitive understanding of all natural processes. Musubi expresses the unique nature and value of each individual life and unites all forms of growth: physical, intellectual, emotional and spiritual. At the same time, it binds together all life in a common purpose: alignment with Kami, so that all that is positive and good in the universe, all that is truly *alive*, can be fulfilled and celebrated. Human society is to be aligned with Kami, so that it is based on compassion, justice, ecological sensitivity and the mutual dependence of all its members. Through these simplest of principles, which are also the hardest to put into practice, true individual liberty is achieved. That freedom is based on security and responsibility in place of self-centered demands and instant gratification, which are social as much as spiritual dead-ends.

Musubi frees the individual from the artificially imposed dogmas and rigid moral laws that lead to hollow observance without understanding, and without compassion for the self or others. However it also frees the individual from the idea that he or she is alone in the universe, separate from other human beings and the forces of nature. And it also frees humanity from the sense that it is above, beyond or set apart from nature, a bleak view of the universe and an increasingly deadly mistake. We learn to think of a forest, in which each individual tree is an equally important contributor to the whole. Or we can return to the idea of *koke musu* ('moss grows'), by which a myriad individual life forms grow together on the face of a rock, unique yet wholly dependent on each other.

It is therefore true that Musubi provides us with a non-mechanistic, non-linear approach to human development, and more importantly the development of everything within nature. Musubi abolishes the division between humanity and 'the rest' of life and exposes it as a human construct, an illusion that blinds us to the truth about ourselves. The division is replaced by a continuum. All forms of life develop in essentially the same way

– *koke musu* – and depend on each other for their continued growth. And all life is continuously being recycled. It follows that everything that promotes and encourages life is therefore inherently good. Anything that stifles or suppresses life is inherently dangerous and destructive.

In Musubi, life spontaneously occurs, organically develops and creatively interacts. Life itself is the only 'cause' and the only 'effect' in the universe. It comes before any man-made system of ethics or law. Or rather, the only systems of ethics and law that are worthwhile or valid are those that are in accord with natural impulses, in other words with Kannagara or the alignment of man and Kami. In this sense, Shinto teaches us to view the world differently from either the three great monotheistic religions or the doctrines of karma found within the Indic traditions.

Kami is the agent of creation in Shinto, but it also pervades everything in the universe. But in marked contrast to the Abrahamic faiths, the obedience to Kami that Shinto demands is obedience to the laws of nature, rather than a demand that we transcend nature. Practitioners of Shinto think first about bequeathing a happier, safer world to future generations, then about what might happen after death. But death and afterlife are always less important than the celebration of living. Ancestors are important because they are still living, in spiritual terms and as expressions of Kami, not because they are physically dead. They express the continuity of life between the generations and also inspire us to continue to develop, spiritually and creatively, and to generate new life. In Shinto, the cycles of life on Earth are more important than any life beyond the world. If we aspire to 'become Kami', then that is an aspiration to fulfill our highest abilities as human beings, rather than leaving our humanity behind us.

Karma, which means 'action' in Sanskrit, is a law of cause and effect by which every action in the universe affects every other action. The soul (described in many different ways, for example *atman* or *jiva*) goes through many earthly incarnations that can cross the boundaries of species, gender, race and caste until it finds enlightenment, usually defined as liberation or *Moksha*. This is a form of escape from *samsara*, the cycle of birth, death and rebirth that is portrayed as a constantly turning wheel. Samsara is, like the 'vale of tears' of the Abrahamic faiths, a state of imperfection and the aim of the spiritual journey is to move beyond it. In most teachings that involve karma, therefore, there is a marked preference for the other-worldly over any existence in the world, however (relatively) unsullied that existence might be. There is a tendency to emphasize asceticism and abstemiousness, in particular abstention from sex, as indicative of withdrawal from the world.

Shinto starts with the assumption that life is by definition good and that this goodness is reflected in the workings of nature (Musubi). Instead of helping us to 'escape' from life and nature, spiritual practice is about learning to understanding them better. Enlightenment means learning to live in a more truly 'natural' way, rather than withdrawing from nature. Alignment with Kami takes place within our earthly lives, rather than through death or a form of 'God-Realization' that moves the soul to an area beyond the human realm. Spiritual awareness helps us to live more fully and more creatively than we might otherwise do. This is because, within Shinto, there are no 'material' and 'spiritual' compartments. These two areas of existence overlap, intersect and are merged, because they flow from the same source: Kami.

Spiritual practice makes us aware of the overlap between the spiritual and material spheres, in the same way that it binds together reason and intuition. We are reminded not to think of the spiritual as something *other*, but as part of ourselves. At the same time, we are enjoined not to confuse an enjoyment of the material world with a *materialistic* worldview. Respect for the material world is respect for life, caring for the environment and thinking generations ahead, rather than merely about the present and the immediate. Materialism, by contrast, is about the accumulation of things and instant gratification. It produces a distorted, unbalanced view of life which is proving to be ecologically destructive as well as destructive to the human psyche. Musubi excludes the mechanistic or fatalistic aspects of karmic teachings, as they have evolved over centuries. But like karma, it emphasizes the interconnectedness of all aspects of life and the continuities between generations. It stresses the position of humanity within the web of life, on which we depend for our survival. And it reminds us that our human intelligence gives us responsibilities instead of arbitrary powers. The most important of these is the responsibility to retain the balance of nature rather than disrupt it with materialistic excess. In the words of Hiroshi Motoyama of the Tamamitsu Shrine:

> The planet Earth is the material manifestation of the Planetary Spirit. This translates to mean that all natural objects and all geographic locations are imbued with their own spirit. Ancient people knew this fact; modern man has forgotten it. It is misguided to think that we can do whatever we want to the nature around us. Earth, stone, trees, tiny insects, all of the things that live together on this planet have spirit.[90]

We see here the ancient Shinto consciousness of nature and the interconnectedness of all life. Yet we see also the Buddhist consciousness that all creatures, including the smallest, have souls of equal worth that must be respected. This principle of *Ahimsa*, the conscious effort to avoid all forms of harm to others, is rooted in Indic spiritual culture and is closely linked to the idea of karma. Harm to others, through negligence, materialism and selfish lack of respect, invariably generates negative karmic patterns. The self-centered individual, who inflicts harm, has not realized him or herself and so is stuck in the repetitive cycle of samsara. Motoyama has written extensively about the principle of karma. However his focus is on its liberating potential, which has at times been neglected by orthodox Buddhist scholarship. He stresses that karma is not merely about fate and destiny, but just as much about self-determination and choice.

To Dr Motoyama, our individuality is a delicate balance of genetic inheritance (or the legacy of the ancestors), environmental influences and the accumulated experience of many lifetimes. Karma becomes a psychotherapeutic tool with which we make sense of our experiences and are able to make appropriate choices. Dr Motoyama uses past life regression as part of his process of healing a client's soul. This goes beyond conventional psychotherapy in that it emphasizes the interconnectedness of life rather than focusing exclusively on the individual. Awareness of past lives can also be interpreted as gaining insight into ancestral experience: a form of spiritual genealogy. Moreover, it allows us to set our ambitions and desires in a wider context and decide what is really important for us.

Karma is thereby transformed into a resource through which we make sense of patterns in our lives by understanding how they were formed. We can, if necessary, break or modify them. This can happen within our present lives, through greater clarity of thinking and self-awareness. We do not have to transcend the world, but merely better understand our place within it. Not only do individuals have karma, but so do peoples, places, landscapes: 'Each nation on earth has its own Spirit, and that Spirit has its own karma'.[91] Through karmic awareness, nations can confront their own past and alter destructive patterns, while maintaining their true nature or essence. The process of political and social reconstruction undergone by Japan after World War II was spiritual as much as it was political and economic. The nation's institutional structure altered, but the nation retained its essence, or its soul – a form of national Musubi, by which continuity and change were successfully tied together.

This view of karma as a means of enriching our emotional lives is thoroughly influenced by Shinto. However it also restores to karma many of its original principles, including respect for the diversity of life and recognition of the ability to change and grow while being true to one's inner nature. Millions of Japanese who follow or are influenced by the Buddhist dharma accept the karmic principle. Because they are also influenced by Shinto, they see karma as empowering and life-affirming, part of our understanding of our true selves. They see awareness of karmic patterns, and the modification of behaviors leading to negative karma, a means of achieving Kannagara: tuning in to the Way of Kami.

Karma is thereby reinterpreted as spiritual Musubi. It is a process of disentangling negative patterns that have emerged, usually through the disruption of natural processes. Understanding of karma allows us to reconnect positive forces and unblock creative energy. For the individual and society alike, karma becomes an aid to growth. Karma and Musubi both arise from the same ancient understanding of the connections between everything in the universe, the underlying unity or ocean of being. It can be said that karma is cerebral or left-brained awareness, while Musubi is right-brained and intuitive. As such, they interact and complement each other. They form the core of the alliance (musubi) of Indic and indigenous Japanese thought, through which both are enriched, but retain their essential qualities. A spiritual union has taken place over centuries between Dharma and Kannagara-no-Michi: they have become intertwined, but remain distinct, occupying different areas of consciousness. As Fujisawa points out, Musubi and Yoga both mean 'union'.[92] Through these parallel processes, the human being connects with processes far greater than the self.

Musubi for the Modern World

The principle of Musubi underlies all of Shinto thought and

practice. It is about observed experience far more than philosophical speculation: observations of patterns within nature, which affect the structures of human society and the relationship between humanity and Kami. Musubi literally *binds together* the social and political with the spiritual domains, just as it unites the world of Kami with the human realm. Awareness of Musubi involves the search for balance. The personal, the social and the ecological are no longer separate compartments. No positive changes can take place in any one of these areas without impacting on all of the others. Conversely, an imbalance in any one of them makes reform of any of the others impossible.

This message, embedded in Shinto teachings, has perhaps never been more relevant to us than today. Globally and locally, we are now contending with the effects of imbalance in virtually every sphere of life. Humans collectively have used only one part of their intelligence, the linear and mechanical, and have forgotten their intuitive and imaginative powers.

By confusing intelligence and creativity with the use of force and arbitrary power, humans are threatening their own lives, as well as (or rather as part of) all other life on the planet. The intelligence that has led to technological progress and scientific discovery could also swallow us up if it is not balanced by intuition and compassion: sympathy with all creatures. Through a limited and selective use of human intelligence, the alliance (Musubi) between humanity and the planet has been broken and the knot (also Musubi) has been untied.

A new, ecological Musubi is therefore needed to reunite the natural world with humankind. This involves human beings learning to respect Great Nature once again and find their own place within it. That in turn means ceasing to regard nature as an *infinite* resource at our disposal to be plundered, molded and undermined at will, but seeing it once again as a *finite* resource, of which we are part, and which we need to work with instead of against. Ecological Musubi is about rediscovering the sacred within nature, and hence within ourselves. We need to relearn to listen to nature's rhythms and compromise and yield to them, instead of striving ceaselessly for a dominance we shall never achieve.

Ecological Musubi, in short, is recognizing that the awe induced by inspiring landscapes is not irrational or superstitious. It is not separate from, but an essential part of, scientific understanding and the use of reason. When we find the sacred in natural formations, we become aware of the hidden powers of nature, to overwhelm us as well as nurture us. We acquire a sense of humility, of our 'smallness' as individuals and as a human race. Yet the same time we become aware of ourselves as part of something far greater than ourselves, *Dai Shizen* to Shinto practitioners and Gaia to many western environmentalists. Both terms express the same idea, the Earth as an organism made up of connected parts. They also express a sense of spiritual affinity with nature, or (in the case of Gaia theory in particular), a wish on the part of secular, scientific human civilization to rediscover the sacred and so complete the circle – the completion of the circle being another meaning of Musubi.

Through the alignment of the scientific and the sacred, human life is enriched by a sense of enchantment that puts dreams of dominance in perspective. Just as importantly, we relearn how to live within the cycle of nature, as ancient, non-technological peoples once knew. Through the concept of *koke musu*, we can also learn from supposedly primitive organisms how to grow in a sustainable way, in alignment with our surroundings rather than choking or overwhelming them by over-replicating ourselves or by exploiting and destroying other ecosystems. We learn to use technology wisely and for the benefit of nature, conscious of ourselves as part of something more (ultimately Kami), rather than as ends in ourselves or the only forms of life that have any importance. That is ecological Musubi. Organic growth is not only about expansion, but also about contraction, not only about stretching boundaries, but also about living within limits.

These polarities, united by Musubi, constantly fluctuate and interact as part of the natural cycle. We see, in the cycle of the seasons, as well as the cycle of any individual's life, the process of expanding and contracting in keeping with natural boundaries. Thus family planning is as much a part of Musubi as reproduction, where it ensures quality of life and access to resources without harming the environment. A balanced or 'steady state' economy is as much a part of Musubi as economic growth: more so, in fact, because it ensures that human activity moves in harmony with other natural processes. Musubi enables us to understand laws of nature that have been absorbed and followed instinctively by peoples supposedly less 'advanced' than modern, technological man who have lived in closer union with Great Nature. True intelligence knows where to stop and true power knows where to yield: this is the ecological lesson of Musubi for humanity today.

The ecological crisis cannot be separated from the political and social structures from which it has arisen, or the assumptions about human society that underlie them. If we try to mark off 'environmental issues' from 'social issues', we are at best putting a temporary sticking plaster on a wound that needs radical surgery. Both are equally 'human' issues and, as a result, they are spiritual or in Shinto terms *Kami issues*. Ecological disharmony is a reflection of social disharmony. Moreover it reflects that disharmony back, as deepening environmental wounds increase the social wounds that first led to ecological destruction. A vicious circle arises from the breakage of the union between society and nature. To restore a virtuous circle, Musubi must also be restored, so that society allies itself with natural principles, instead of ignoring or defying nature. This means rethinking our ideas about progress so that they cease to be impersonal and mechanistic and reflect deeper, more primal human needs. Thus the ties of affection, friendship and community, the need for tranquility and communing with Great Nature, mean more than the accumulation of commodities as ends in themselves. It is through these, and not simply through consuming, that individuals find their true selves.

A social Musubi restores to humanity the concept of organic growth (and contraction) in place of the present pursuit of unfettered economic growth - whatever the social and ecological costs, let alone the psychic and spiritual effects. The over-exploitation of finite resources has led, quite logically, to the unequal distribution of those resources: the concentration of wealth in a few hands and the corresponding impoverishment of millions. The result is that, for the most part, the greater the levels of wealth generated, the more unequal the distribution of that wealth and the greater the relative impoverishment of sections of the population. The social and environmental consequences of impoverishment then counteract most of the benefits of material and technological progress. The political consequences, in turn, work against peace and stability by encouraging (among other things) terrorism and fundamentalism. These are the wrong reactions to global injustice, or the suppression of cultural or religious identities. But they can be understood as part of the vicious cycle arising from the absence of human solidarity, the Musubi or common bond that unites us as human beings.

When the Earth's resources are seen as commodities to be competed for, rather than as fruits to be harvested and enjoyed, there is every incentive for conflict between human societies, fighting for a share of the spoils, and within those societies, between those who possess and those who are deprived of resources. The idea of a shared human endeavor, and a common interest between humanity and the rest of nature, is lost. Thus there is a direct connection between the despoliation of nature and a narrow view of economic expansion at all costs. This view is based on a loss of a sense of the sacred. When natural resources are viewed as commodities, to be extracted, fought over and competed for at will, they are objectified. They are stripped of their spiritual qualities – their *Kami nature* - for solely materialistic ends. Social iniquity, in other words, arises when the alignment of material and spiritual forces has been lost or forgotten.

Therefore it follows that the restoration of social Musubi is about far more than a choice between 'capitalism' and 'socialism'. For these (and other 'isms') are based on the same materialistic assumptions, the same belief that economic growth can, in itself, generate human well-being and that takes place without reference to any other process within nature. Where they differ is over the primary instrument of growth: the market or the state, the individual or the collective. Social Musubi places both individual initiative (the 'capitalist' ethic) and collective well-being (the 'socialist' ethic) in the wider context of co-operation between humans and their environment. It is a form of human ecology, in which society is organized in according to the cycles - and limits - of nature. This means respect for the freedom of the individual and his or her right to grow and develop full creative potential. Yet that freedom is inseparable from a sense of solidarity with fellow human beings and responsibility for them. The two principles are bound together because they ensure social balance. There is, then, no point in ideological shifts from 'right' to 'left' within a spectrum that ignores large areas of human and ecological experience. It is that spectrum itself which deprives humans of the spiritual insights we need to fashion a more sustainable world order.

Social Musubi reunites modern humanity with the web of life and so makes environmental awareness the primary social concern. Crucially, however, social Musubi also places modern humans in the context of accumulated human experience of eons, ancestral wisdom, and our responsibility towards future genera-tions. These two lines connect us first with other living systems on the planet and secondly with our ancestors and descendents. As such, they can be seen as forms of horizontal and vertical Musubi, tying us into responsibilities for the present and the future and connecting us to the insights and values of our forebears so that we can apply them in a modern context.

For social harmony to be restored, economics needs to be reconciled with nature, including human nature and so returned to its original ancient Greek meaning, 'the law of the household', or good housekeeping.[93] The house in question is the Earth and its inhabitants. The problem with modern economics is that it has become an abstract science, removed from the needs of human beings and the environments in which they live. Like much of the western Enlightenment tradition from which it emerged, economics has been taken over by its linear, mechanistic aspect, confusing scientific reason with narrow, statistical abstraction. Hence it has lost its holistic dimension, which recognizes that human societies develop organically, in harmony with the environments that nurture them, and with all sections of those societies working towards a common end.

The result of economics closing itself off from other areas of life has been far from rational. It has meant that people – and ecosystems – are forced to conform to overarching economic 'models', instead of those models being constructed in response to human and ecological need. Furthermore, it has led to the rise of a superstitious form of market fundamentalism, based on appeals to the 'hidden hand' or the 'iron law' of the market, rather than recognizing that markets are human constructs. A social Musubi means accepting that markets are made by and for humanity and that we are not passive playthings of abstract 'market forces'. Looked at objectively, it is remarkable that such superstitions should be accepted so uncritically by rational men and women. This demonstrates that, far from abolishing superstition, the absence of a spiritual dimension raises it to new heights of folly.

Within the Shinto tradition, there is Kami power associated with business, prosperity and the market. These are as much endowed with vital energy as any other human activity, and by extension any activity within nature. They are expressions of human intelligence and the creative power that brings humans into alignment with Kami. But they are not set apart from, or above, other human activities, any more than human society is set apart from the other activities of nature. Social Musubi should therefore be a process of integration: of economics with the human spirit and human society with the spirit of nature. The present economic system is one of disequilibrium and imbalance. That is why it lurches from crisis to crisis, why its effects are increasingly devastating to the environment (without which there could be no economics) and why, despite all the wealth it generates, it fails to satisfy human need and instead creates stress, discontent and neurosis on a massive scale.

The ethic of co-operation means that individuals are not viewed as isolated, autonomous 'atoms', lacking connection with or obligation to each other. In place of this bleak model of narrow individualism (which has dominated modern political economy, especially in the west), we substitute the idea of cells in the body, each one uniquely individual and of equal importance, but each one existing in the context of the whole. In the same way that the cells of a healthy human body replicate, fade and give way to new cells, so a functioning human society changes and renews itself whilst retaining its identity and integrity. Similarly, a society founded on Musubi works constantly for the alignment, rather than opposition between, social classes, occupations and interest groups. When areas of the human body are in conflict, or cannot communicate with each other, the result is illness, paralysis and possibly death.

A functioning human society is about healing divisions between that society's components rather than encouraging divisions or conflicts. More than that, it is about maintaining a climate in which divisions are less likely to arise. That means honoring all sections of society: the craftsman as much as the financier, the artist, writer or musician as much as the industrialist or the accountant, the scholar as much as the sportsman, the female as much as the male, the homemaker as much as the careerist. All these areas of a society's life work together, for the benefit of the whole society. None is worth 'less' than the other and none is in competition with any of the others. And nor, it should be pointed out, need any of these abilities or roles be mutually exclusive. There is no reason why an individual should not occupy many or all of them and no reason why these roles should be confined wholly to certain sectors of society. It is healthy that there should be as much interaction and overlap as possible, since from the Shinto perspective, all are expressions of the creative Kami and all benefit the individual and society alike. They are social ecosystems and, as with the ecosystems of the natural world, they connect with each other in subtle and unexpected ways, without the arbitrary divisions imposed by mechanistic thinking. Social Musubi views human society as an organism, made up of parts that work together and complement each other.

The principle of co-operation extends logically from individual nations, cultures and ethnic groups towards the entire world community. The environment, after all, is not restrained by man-made boundaries or cultural differences. Indeed the idea of Musubi could be said to provide the elusive 'new paradigm' or model for relations between the world's peoples. Musubi means alliance, knot, or partnership, which brings together disparate forces and ties them into a shared identity and common purpose. At the same time, their original identities and qualities remain intact: they are enhanced by a connection to something more than the self.

Musubi also means growth in the sense of *growing together* peacefully and in a state of natural balance. This should be the principal aim of international relations. Within a nation, or community based on shared values (culture, language, religious or tribal allegiance), the aim should be should be consensus, with the organs of the 'body politic' working in harmony rather than conflict. This can be called national Musubi. International Musubi applies this concept of unity-in-diversity to the Earth as a whole. In the same way as the biosphere can only function if its ecosystems are connected and work together, the world community can only work without conflict if there is open and equitable communication between its component peoples.

The biosphere is composed of diverse parts that work together to give us the planet we recognize and need: they are distinct, and yet they are one, unique yet part of the Whole. Equally, the *ethnosphere*[94] is based on cultural, ethnic and social diversity that needs to be respected if there is to be any balance between the Earth's human populations – and without such balance, ecological and social Musubi cannot be achieved. That diversity is part of a wider human unity. But the suppression of any part of that diversity will have the same effect as the suppression or abuse of an organ of the human body. The resulting conflicts, wars and loss of often vital ancient wisdom mirror the symptoms of disease, and they also inflict profound ecological scars on the Earth.

International Musubi extends the idea of preserving biological diversity to the preservation of *human* diversity. One is an extension of the other. Preserving the diversity of human cultures ensures that as wide a variety of sources of wisdom remain at the disposal of humanity as a whole. Respecting diversity is also the most effective way to achieve human unity. Conflict arises when one culture, or economic system, becomes too dominant and attempts to impose its values on others. The false assumption of superior wisdom leads to the abuse of that wisdom and the misuse of human intelligence to destructive, self-defeating ends.

In nature as a whole, and in the human race, the attempt to

impose a monoculture is invariably disruptive. It creates, at best, the illusion of unity, masking disorder and dysfunction. Musubi is about partnership between and reconciliation of different principles, so that they serve the same end. It is not about one principle triumphing over or striking down another. Musubi is the tying of a knot, in which both cords are intertwined, rather than one dominating the other. That is the 'model' for relationships between human groups that Shinto can now offer the modern world. To those used to aggression, it might seem 'utopian', but it is in fact far simpler than the negative patterns that have arisen through a failure to tune in to Kami energy.

Shinto has always recognized that differences between faith traditions disguise an essential unity between them. The immense variety of deities, tenets and practices that exist within human consciousness are all expressions of Kami. Humanity's spiritual quest crosses all divisions of race and culture. Throughout human history, it has changed and evolved, but remained constant. This is why Shinto does not claim to have a monopoly of truth. It is a sensibility and a pattern of thought that has developed in the context of the Japanese people's experience and history, as well as the landscape and ecology of Japan, with which it is intertwined. Yet it also has a universal relevance to us in making sense of our world. It helps us to understand that the spiritual journey passes through diverse landscapes in the attempt to reach the same place.

Without volubility or aggression, Shinto challenges the concept of monopolistic religions and similar secular ideologies. It takes for granted the idea that there are many paths to the truth and many versions of the divine. All of these are reflections of Kami, which is the principle of life rather than a specific deity. How Kami is approached is far less important than the approach itself. That can take place through individual contemplation as much as collective worship, a sudden and powerful sense of the sacred in trees, mountains or fields as much as prolonged meditation on a single object or Mantra.

Because Kami includes, but is not the same as, 'gods' or 'God', there is no reason why an atheist or agnostic should not access Kami energy. This is provided that he or she is a genuine 'humanist', who believes in human responsibilities rather than only human power. Such a humanist is far more likely to be able to approach Kami than a religious believer, of whatever faith, who seeks to impose his or her doctrines on others by force.[95]

From this it follows that spiritual Musubi is part of the reconciliation between humanity and the Earth, and hence humanity and Kami. Spiritual Musubi is the tying together of disparate strands of human spiritual practice, so that a unity between them is understood as their diversity is respected and preserved. The same rules apply to spiritual systems as to systems within nature and the organization of human society. All arise from the same source, Kami, and exist in a state of mutual dependence. Without the cultivation of the spirit, there can be no sense of security within individual human beings and nor can human society function along harmonious lines.

The spiritual sense connects human beings with each other and with Great Nature. If that connection is broken, through divisive ideologies and religions, or through humans misunderstanding their own powers, then the biosphere is in danger from pollution, conflict and unrestrained economic expansion. When the connections between the spiritual and natural worlds are forgotten, humans turn against Great Nature and therefore against themselves. When they are remembered and valued, then humans are at ease with themselves and able to fulfill their potential. Through spiritual Musubi, men and women can ally themselves with Kami. This alliance should be reflected in their treatment of the planet as much as in their relations with fellow human beings.

Musubi becomes a process of healing by which we let go of negative patterns of living and thinking and by doing so connect with our essential selves. Healing takes place at each of the three levels of consciousness – ecological, social and personal, at the same time. Each process, each limb of the Shinto triad, interacts with and depends on each of the others. At times, personal considerations predominate, at others social issues and at others the process of looking after and nurturing our world. But all three are equal and all three are intertwined. Musubi dispels the individual's false consciousness of the self as separate from others and from the world, in a perpetual state of competition with fellow humans. True individual consciousness is being, literally, *alive to* connections with fellow humans, the natural world and the spiritual force that runs through everything in the universe. For the Shinto practitioner, that is how Kami is brought into contact with humankind.

The idea of 'letting go' of negative influences is linked to the Shinto view of human nature. According to the Way of Kami, human nature, like all of nature, is in essence good. Goodness, in this context, means the ability to follow the simple natural laws of growth, contraction and transformation. Pollution is every influence that disrupts this natural flow, every action or thought process that removes humanity from nature, every oppressive action, everything that damages the planet. It is the death force that destroys life and ends the process of organic growth. Above all, it is identified with misalignment or imbalance. In human society, and within the self, it arises when consciousness of nature and Kami is lost or willfully neglected. Thus Shinto extends the idea of ecology from concern for our surroundings to concern for the mind and spirit. Our psychic well-being is part of planetary well-being.

Sympathy and love are natural human qualities in Shinto. They contrast with hatred, anger and greed, which are external forces arising from loss of Kami-consciousness. They are akin to diseases that infect and disrupt the human body when the immune response is low. Spiritual practice is the treatment of psychic wounds, the re-tying of knots, the realignment of natural forces. It reminds us of our true position in the universe. From the perspective of Shinto, co-operation is a natural human characteristic. Humans co-operate with each other just as the cells in the body of any living organism co-operate and human communities need all the characteristics of a living organism to function effectively. This is the opposite of the western, post-Enlightenment perspective that has become orthodox opinion and is routinely used to rationalize the aggressive and competitive aspects of human behavior.

Freedom *and* co-operation, choice *and* obligation, are the Musubi of personal growth. An over-emphasis on freedom produces social disorder and psychic wounds, as individuals fail to become social beings and suffer a loss of spiritual awareness. The result is materialistic craving and attachment, which are the opposite of freedom. Likewise, an over-emphasis on group loyalty produces tyrannical collectivism and restrictive social conformity. This is the opposite of co-operation, because it creates a climate of resentment, in which human potential is crushed instead of being allowed to develop. Musubi is the synthesis of these two polarities of co-operation and freedom. They are bound together to create the right conditions for human life to advance.

Jean Herbert wisely concluded that Musubi 'allows for the combining of tradition and progress'. Through it, Shinto is able 'to retain its traditions and adapt continuously' at the same time.[97] Applied to human society, the division between change and flux, the conservative and the radical, is resolved through a union of these apparent opposites. For modern humanity, the lesson of Musubi is that they are not opposites at all, but preconditions of human fulfillment. To achieve that balance, we need to look at progress from a different angle. We have tended to view it as a straight line, moving inexorably forward as it erases all that has gone before. In practice, this is a narrow vision that limits and damages us, because it excludes so much of human experience. A more expansive vision of progress is a continuously revolving spiral that integrates past, present and future. This includes all living systems and all stages of the evolutionary cycle, giving each life a context and a meaning.

Musubi gives us an alternative vision of growth that is about more than accumulating possessions and exploiting nature. We have the chance to re-learn and apply to the modern world our primal understanding of growth as an organic process, in partnership with the natural world and our fellow men and women. There is surely no better way to address the psychic, social and ecological problems that color this present phase of human existence.

Chapter Six: Sympathy With All Creatures

What, then, is Shinto? In the final analysis, it is a pure expression of human intuition. ... It is the universal inheritance of mankind and is the root of human existence.
Nahum Stiskin[98]

The Shinto practitioner in the modern city is expected to have as much awareness of the power and fragility of nature as a Native American or Kalahari Bushman. The continued existence of Shinto proves that ethos of living as if nature mattered does not require abandoning the accoutrements and technologies of modern living – which are themselves products of centuries of accumulated experience. It is not the technology that matters, but the ways in which it is used. If it is used to bolster human arrogance and to detach humanity from nature, then it precipitates social and environmental crisis. If it is used to integrate humanity with nature, then it has the potential to liberate us from the worst aspects of civilization.

Such liberation need not involve social or technological regression. On the contrary, it means a shift of emphasis in the way we use that skill and knowledge, so that we co-operate with Great Nature rather than trying to compete against it. This ethic of co-operation should be replicated in human relationships. That is the first premise of Kannagara-no-Michi, the awareness of humanity's relationship with the rest of nature and the individual's relationship with the rest of humanity.

This is true knowledge, true spiritual evolution. There is nothing 'new' about it because it reflects some of the most ancient insights of humanity, going back to the Age of the Heavenly Kami, when the first spiritual impulses were felt. Yet the idea of thinking in circles rather than restrictive straight lines makes sense in the light of recent science, which challenges the narrow, linear assumptions of the recent past. The same applies to Shinto's sense of humility before the universe and the natural world, and the understanding that all forms of life are connected, that we are each other as well as our limited selves.

We need the insights of Shinto more than ever as we become aware of the consequences of our disconnection from Great Nature and each other. The increasing awareness that something is wrong with our form of social organization, that its values and priorities are false and give no ultimate satisfaction or security is really an awareness that we have wandered away from the Kannagara, the Way of Attunement to Kami. Environmental pollution, social injustice and the vast disparities of wealth between different regions of the world are material manifestations of a deeper spiritual malaise.

Far from trivializing these problems, this spiritual perspective compels us to work on them internally as well as externally, in the private and personal as well as collective and public spheres. The alienation from nature, from work, from each other that is at the root of so many conflicts at so many levels arises from lack of balance. It stems from an over-concentration on the material at the expense of the spiritual, the self as an isolated unit instead of shared human and planetary needs. Spiritual practice in the Shinto tradition is therefore about re-learning that sense of the *whole* that ancient civilizations possessed (and indigenous cultures retain today) and marrying it to the needs of our literate, city-based culture. This is the form of Musubi that Shinto can help us towards – Musubi in the sense of a union of rational and intuitive powers, producing a more balanced relationship between humanity and the planet.

These insights are by no means limited to the native faith of Japan. They lie deep within our consciousness, whatever our cultural roots, because they are reflections of the original, 'nameless' religion of the earliest human communities. Shinto is a fragment of that nameless religion that has survived millennia of social changes, evolving but not surrendering its inner nature. That is its value to modern men and women. As the Shinto scholar Sokyo Ono has expressed it:

> *People of all races and climes cannot help but express gratitude to the spirits of the land and of nature [and] to their ancestors. In so far as they recognize this feeling within them, they cannot but understand the spirit of Shinto, and find in it an undeniable truth which supports and heightens man's noblest values. Shinto ... possesses a universality which can enrich the lives of all people everywhere.*[99]

The simplest rule and most profound teaching of Shinto is *Mono no aware*, 'sympathy with all creatures', respect for and celebration of all life. This is the earliest spiritual principle of all and it is also the most compelling for our times.

Notes

1. 'The Litany of the Tree', from Stuart D.B. Picken, *Shinto: Meditations for Revering the Earth* (Berkeley, CA: Stone Bridge Press, 2002). Stuart Picken is a Scottish Presbyterian minister who has lived in Japan and studied Shinto extensively.

2. The sun, the center of Shinto worship, is also a symbol of continuity and change, both because it sets and rises and because fluctuations of solar activity can profoundly affect conditions on Earth.

3. *Kojiki* Sections I-IV, translated by Basil Hall Chamberlain, with annotations by W.G. Aston (Boston, MA: Tuttle, 1982). I have remained almost entirely faithful to Chamberlain's translation, except that I have substituted the original word Kami for Aston's use of 'Deity'. The translation was first completed in 1882, with updated versions in 1919 and 1920.

4. Version of the *Nihongi* translated by W.G. Aston (London: George Allen and Unwin, 1956), quoted in Barbara C. Sproull, *Primal Myths: Creating the World* (London: Rider, 1980), p.212. The *Nihongi* often contains multiple versions of the same story, in which there are different emphases and varying sequences of events.

5. The Master-of-the-August-Center-of-Heaven [Ame-no-minaka-nushi-no-kami] is, presumably, beyond gender as the supreme balancing force within the universe. The use of the masculine pronoun to refer to him – and the other spontaneously arising Kami deities – is based on convention rather than the ascription of clearly masculine characteristics.

6. Onogoro is a mythical island. However the *Kojiki-den*, the detailed commentary on the *Kojiki* by Motoori Norinaga (1730-1801 CE) claims that it is one of the small islands close to Awajishima. This places it in the eastern region of the Seto

Inland Sea, between the islands of Honshu and Shikoku.

7. W.G. Aston (tr.), *Nihongi: Chronicles of Japan from the Earliest Times to A.D. 67* (North Clarendon, Vermont: Tuttle Publishing, 1972), p.21. This translation first appeared in 1896.

8. *Kojiki*, Section XI, pp. 51-2

9. The word Tsunami literally means 'Harbor-Wave'

10. M. Anesaki, *History of Japanese Religion* (1930). Quoted in A.C. Underwood, *Shintoism: The Indigenous Religion of Japan* (London: The Epworth Press, 1934).

11. The 'Land of Yomi', a shadowy realm of the dead similar to the Greek Hades, is mentioned in the early stages of the *Kojiki* and *Nihongi*, but does not play a prominent role in Shinto belief and practice.

12. Jean Herbert, *Shinto: The Fountainhead of Japan* (London: George Allen and Unwin, 1967), p.65. Herbert is quoting from Akira Nakanishi of Chuo University, Tokyo.

13. See http://eos.kokugakuin.ac.jp/modules

14. Herbert, pp.26-7

15. Herbert, p.27

16. Herbert, p.60

17. Herbert, p.60

18. For a comprehensive account of Haitian Vodou and its hidden spiritual teachings, see Maya Deren, *Divine Horsemen: The Living Gods of Haiti* (Kingston, New York: McPherson and Company, 2004). First published by Thames and Hudson, London and New York, 1953.

19. Herbert, p.61

20. A Grand Master is the head of a philosophical school, community or family of Shinto practitioners. The term 'family' in this context includes friendship and fellowship through shared beliefs and practices, as well as blood ties. Thus a Grand Master is a higher position than a Guji (senior priest) or a Kannushi, although Gujia and Kannushi can

make just as creative and powerful contributions to Shinto. In many cases, the title of Grand Master is hereditary. Kanchou is the word used for Grand Master in Yamakage Shinto and some other schools. It can also be loosely translated as 'Head Priest', 'High Priest' or 'Superintendent Priest'.

21. Motohisa Yamakage [edited by Paul de Leeuw and Aidan Rankin], *The Essence of Shinto: Japan's Spiritual Heart* (Tokyo: Kodansha International, 2007), pp.56-8. In the English language edition of this book, Grand Master Yamakage is referred to according to European custom as Motohisa Yamakage (the given name preceding the family name).

22. Yamakage, pp.56-8

23. Herbert, p.26

24. Herbert, p.30

25. *Nihongi*, pp.14-16

26. Herbert, p.31

27. Chikao Fujisawa, PhD., *Zen and Shinto: The Story of Japanese Philosophy* (New York: Philosophical Library, Inc., 1959), p.16

28. Fujisawa, p.16

29. A parallel process is the confusion of the ideology individualism with individuality and self-realization.

30. Serge King, 'The Way of the Adventurer' in Shirley Nicholson (ed.), *Shamanism: An Expanded View of Reality* (Wheaton, IL: Quest Books, 1987), p. 202

31. See, for example, Rupert Sheldrake, *The Rebirth of Nature: The Greening of Science and God* (Rochester, VT: Inner Traditions, 1994) and David Bohm, *Wholeness and the Implicate Order* (London: Routledge, 2002).

32. Fujisawa, p.16

33. In this context, the 'resignation' of Emperor Hirohito as a Kami (or a representative of Kami power on Earth) after 1945 seems less surprising.

34. Herbert, p.24

35. Herbert, p.25
36. The Kannushi is traditionally a male role, because of social convention rather than any specific teaching. Today, there are a growing number of female Kannushi.
37. Herbert, p.25
38. 'It' would have been a better rendering, because the creative power of Kami transcends gender. It is possible that the translation of Yoshida that Herbert read was influenced by Christian assumptions, so that Kami as Creator was identified too strongly with the Christian image of God. Herbert (who was free of such preconceptions) does not speculate about this.
39. *Naka-ima*, literally 'middle now'.
40. Quoted in Herbert, p.25
41. Herbert, p.25
42. See 'Shinto's View of Nature',
   www.jinjahoncho.or.jp/en/view/
43. Herbert, p.25
44. Herbert, p.25
45. One eminent Guji and scholar cited by Herbert, Yoshiharu Amabe, also 'stresses the difference between the actual real and full Kami, such as Amaterasu-o-mi-kami as a Solar Goddess, Creator of the Universe, and the personified Kami, such as the same Amaterasu-o-mi-kami viewed only as Ancestor' (Herbert, p.30). Clearly, even archetypes can be viewed through different aspects, which have different powers and strengths – a bit like radio waves of different frequencies, some stronger or easier to receive than others.
46. In this sense, they closely resemble the Greco-Roman, Germanic and Celtic deities of Europe.
47. Herbert, p.65
48. Herbert, p.31. It is also worth noting that in Norse mythology (which in many ways resembles early Shinto), several major deities including Odin, Thor, Freyr (or Frey), Heimdall and

Notes

Loki, are destroyed in Ragnarok: the final destiny or 'twilight' of the Gods, after which the universe is renewed.

49. Herbert, p.25

50. Herbert, p.25. The list is drawn from Motoori's *Kojiki-den* commentary.

51. The Way according to Kami: see Chapter Four.

52. Herbert, p.25

53. *Himorogi* and *iwasaka* also mean respectively 'place of worship' and 'small stone'. This reflects the role of sacred trees as the most ancient places of worship and the fact the sacred enclosures were – and often still are – composed of circles of stones.

54. According to Fujisawa, '[the] *himorogi* contains in its bosom the solar energy which comes into full play, thanks to the operation of *musubi* dialectics' (quoted in Herbert, p.94).

55. Herbert, p.30

56. Herbert, p.30

57. This phrase is taken from the spiritual teachings of the English mystic Henry Thomas Hamblin (1873-1958). See. www.hamblintrust.org.uk

58. Quoted in Herbert, p.70

59. Herbert, p.33

60. William Gleason, *The Spiritual Foundations of Aikido* (Rochester, Vermont: Inner Traditions/Bear and Company, 1995), pp.49-50

61. John Keats, 'Ode on a Grecian Urn', 1819.

62. See Brian Bates, *The Wisdom of the Wyrd: Teachings for today from our ancient past* (London: Rider, 1996).

63. See Guji Yukitaka Yamamoto's spiritual autobiography, *Kami no Michi: The Life And Thought Of A Shinto Priest*, on the website of the Tsubaki Grand Shrine of America, Granite Falls, WA: www.tsubakishrine.org/kaminomichi Guji Yamamoto has brought Shinto teachings and worship to North America and made them directly accessible to non-

155

Japanese. He and Guji Yamakage (who has done the same in Europe) are, as far as I am aware, alone in this among Japanese Shinto Masters.

64. Yamamoto, as above.

65. Yamamoto.

66. Herbert, p.70

67. Herbert, p.70

68. Herbert, p.70

69. Herbert, p.70

70. Yamamoto

71. Yamamoto

72. Quoted in Herbert, p.67. From *The Spirit of Shinto Mythology* (Tokyo, 1939). James Mason, an American, also wrote *The Meaning of Shinto* in 1935. It was reprinted by the Matsuri Foundation of Canada in 2002.

73. W.G. Aston, *Shinto: The Way of the Gods* (London: Longman, 1905), pp.20-1

74. R.D. Laing, *The Politics of Experience and The Bird of Paradise* (Harmondsworth: Penguin New Edition, 1990).

75. Herbert, pp.67-8

76. Herbert, p.68

77. Herbert, p.231

78. Herbert, p.67

79. Kami interact with all of nature, not just humans. However it is – at least as far as we know – only humans who have been able to develop a clearly defined consciousness of Kami. Or, expressed in less human-centered terms, Shinto practice is designed primarily for humans to be brought into contact with Kami.

80. Yamamoto: see www.tsubakishrine.org/kaminomichi

81. Sarangerel Odigan, *Riding Windhorses: A Journey into the Heart of Mongolian Shamanism* (Rochester, VT: Destiny Books, 2000), pp.3-4

82. Yamato, as above.

83. Yamakage, pp.125-6
84. Yamakage, pp.125-6
85. Yamakage, p.126
86. Yamakage, p.127
87. Herbert, p.68
88. Herbert likens Musubi to the concept of *élan vital* posited by French philosopher Henri Bergson in his book *Creative Evolution*. Élan Vital is an animating principle closely allied to the development of consciousness, in which the material and spiritual dimensions intersect.
89. Herbert, p.68
90. Hiroshi Motoyama, PhD., *Karma and Reincarnation: The Key to Spiritual Enlightenment* [edited and translated by Rande Brown Ouchi] (London: J. Piatkus, 1992), p.66
91. Motoyama, p.61
92. Fujisawa, p.22
93. From the words *oikos*, house, or household, and *nomos*, law, or rule.
94. See Wade Davis, PhD., 'On Preserving the Diversity of the Ethnosphere', *Shaman's Drum Journal*, No 80, 2009. http://shamansdrum.org
95. The same, of course, applies to a doctrinaire atheist who denies that there is any spiritual dimension in nature and tries to impose this distorted version of rationalism as a new creed.
96. See Chapter 3
97. Herbert, p.68
98. Nahum Stiskin, *The Looking-Glass God: Shinto, Yin-Yang and a Cosmology for Today* (Brookline, MA: Autumn Press Incorporated, 1972), p.150
99. Sokyo Ono, *Shinto: The Kami Way* (Boston, MA: Tuttle, 1962), pp.11-12

Shinto Glossary

Amaterasu, Sun Goddess; solar deity or Kami; ancestor of humanity; life-giving power or origin of all life.

Bosatsu, Buddha, Buddhist deity or icon that may be venerated at Shinto shrine.

Dai Shizen, Great Nature: object of reverence for Shinto practitioners, sometimes viewed as Kami deity (q.v.), more usually as expression of Kami energy and power.

Dogu, Jomon (q.v.) effigy made from clay and viewed as repository of divine or cosmic power.

Guji, senior Kannushi. Often applied to the leader of a shrine. (q.v.).

Himorogi, sacred tree.

Ichirei Shikon, principle of 'One Spirit, Four Souls'.

Ie, extended family group.

Izanagi and Izanami, primal twins (male and female respectively): Kami deities who fashioned the Earth and perhaps gave the universe its present structure.

Jinja, shrine.

Jinja Honcho, Shrine Association: a decentralized federation to which most (but by no means all) Shinto shrines are affiliated.

Jomon, earliest distinctive Japanese civilization, 14000-400 BCE.

Kami, creative energy, spiritual power or vital force animating the universe, akin to Mana in Polynesia; powers latent in nature, humanity and the inner self; deities embodying cosmic, earthly or psychic energies. Grand Master Yamakage Motohisa groups the Kami deities into three categories: Amatsukami (Heavenly Kami), Kunitsukami (earthly Kami) and Yaoyoruzo no Kami (Myriad Other Kami).

Kami no Michi, Way of Kami

Kamidana, household shrine.

Kanchou, Grand Master, or head of a Shinto school of thought, community or family.

Kannagara, process of 'tuning in' to divine consciousness; 'way' or flow of natural energy.

Kannagara no Michi, Way According to Kami.

Kannushi, Shinto 'priest': a spiritual leader and facilitator of contact with Kami.

'Koke musu', 'moss grows': saying that expresses principle of Musubi (q.v.) or organic growth linked to spiritual evolution.

Kojiki, Record of Ancient Matters, 712 CE.

Kokoro, heart or center of spiritual awareness/Kami consciousness.

Michi, Way or spiritual path.

Mi-itsu, intrinsic power ('lofty authority') of Kami deities.

Misogi, purification ritual.

Mono no aware, principle of 'sympathy with all creatures'; reverence for life.

Musubi, organic or sustainable growth; principle and process of physical, spiritual and natural evolution; underlying life principle; union, alignment or binding together (social, spiritual or physical). Also applied to deities (Kami) associated with sustainable or natural growth.

Naobi, Spirit that contains four souls, representing aspects of nature or psychological traits.

Nihongi (or *Nihon Shoki*), Chronicles of Japan, 720 CE.

Norito, invocation or prayer.

Reikon, whole spiritual being, consisting of 'One Spirit and Four Souls'.

Sakaki (Cleyera Japonica), evergreen tree indigenous to Japan and the Korean peninsula. In Shinto, it is often a sacred tree or portal for Kami energy.

Shimenawa, length of knotted rope demarcating sacred space, especially area around sacred tree.

Shinboku, sacred tree; tree in which divine power (Kami energy) resides or through which it can be accessed.

Shintai, 'body of Kami': a representation of the divine principle that can be a tree, river, mountain or other natural formation, but is equally likely to be a simple human-made object of clay, glass, wood, paper, etc. Often a mirror is used as a *shintai*, because it reflects light and is associated with Amaterasu (q.v.).

Shintoku, specific powers or influences of Kami deities.

Takama-no-hara, High Plane of Heaven; superior level of consciousness.

Tama (or *Mitama*), soul, spirit, essential quality of any living being (or Kami deity). Divided into *Aramitama* (turbulent or violent soul), *Nigimitama* (calm or tranquil soul), *Sakimitama* (creative or life-affirming soul) and *Kushimitama* (mysterious or transcendent soul). These 'Four Souls' are complementary and interdependent, because they represent aspects of the universe, the environment and the psychological make-up of humans or other beings.

Tomoe, symbol of the dynamic spirit as three connected 'waves': these represent the visible aspects of the soul - excluding the *Kushimitama*, because it is hidden and mysterious. The Term Mitsu-Tomoe (Triple-Comma) is also often used to describe this symbol.

Ujigami, ancestral or guardian deities of families or clans, villages or localities. Probably the earliest types of Kami deity invoked by Shinto practitioners.

Wa, state of balance, calm or equanimity; also ancient name for Japan in Chinese texts.

Yomi (Land of), shadow-world or underworld associated with the souls of the dead (especially in early Shinto).

Yorishiro, object that attracts and/or embodies sacred energies.